The Flavors of

BON APPÉTIT

2002

Caramelized-Nectarine
Shortcakes with Sour Cream (page 195)

The Flavors of
BON APPÉTIT
2002

from the Editors of Bon Appétit

Condé Nast Books • Clarkson Potter/Publishers

New York

For *Bon Appétit* Magazine

Barbara Fairchild, *Editor-in-Chief*
Kim Upton, *Editor, Bon Appétit Books*
Marcy MacDonald, *Editorial Business Manager*
Carri Marks, *Editorial Production Director*
Lynne Hartung, *Editorial Production Manager*
Sybil Shimazu Neubauer, *Editorial Administrator*
Joy Whittemore McCann, *Associate Editor*
Jordana Ruhland, *Editorial Associate*
Marcia Hartmann Lewis, *Editorial Support*
Norman Kolpas, *Text*
H. Abigail Bok, *Copy Editor*
Gaylen Ducker Grody, *Research*
Elizabeth A. Matlin, *Index*

For Condé Nast Books

Lisa Faith Phillips, *Vice President and General Manager*
Tom Downing, *Direct Marketing Director*
Deborah Williams, *Operations Director*
Peter Immediato, *Business Manager*
Fianna Reznik, *Direct Marketing Assistant*
Eric Levy, *Inventory Assistant*

Design: Monica Elias and Ph.D

Front Jacket: Chicken and Root Vegetable Stew (page 66)
Facing Page: Top: Quick Chicken and Olive Empanadas (page 18)
　　　　　　　　　Middle: Sea Bass with Moroccan Salsa (page 82)
　　　　　　　　　Bottom: Old-fashioned Coconut Cake (page 196)

Published by Clarkson Potter/Publishers, New York, New York.
Member of the Crown Publishing Group, a division of Random House, Inc.

CLARKSON N. POTTER is a trademark and POTTER and colophon are registered trademarks of Random House, Inc.

Printed in the United States of America

Library of Congress Cataloging-in-Publication Data is available upon request.

ISBN 0-609-61064-3

10 9 8 7 6 5 4 3 2 1

FIRST EDITION

Condé Nast Web Address: epicurious.com
Bon Appétit Books Web Address: bonappetitbooks.com
Random House Web Address: randomhouse.com

Contents

Introduction

Like a loving touch, good food—especially when served with friendship—has the power to comfort. No wonder, then, that a home-cooked meal can be just as welcome during challenging times as it is at life's happiest moments.

As this—the ninth annual volume of *The Flavors of Bon Appétit*—vividly demonstrates, comfort foods can come in many forms. Frequently, we categorize them as home-style dishes with roots in America's heartland. You'll find a bounty of such recipes on the pages that follow, from Buttermilk Fried Chicken (page 71) to Beef Stew with Winter Root Vegetables (page 42) to Mashed Potatoes with Spinach and Cheese (page 137) to Banana Cream Pie with Chocolate-Chip-Cookie Crust (page 167). Nearly as often, however, we turn for soothing to popular ethnic dishes that we have adopted as our own: favorites as diverse as Mexican-inspired Smoky Black Bean Dip (page 12), Classic Spaghetti and Meatballs (page 118) or Bistro French Fries with Parsley and Garlic (page 134).

Banana Cream Pie with Chocolate-Chip-Cookie Crust (page 167)

Not surprisingly, the most indulgent of ingredients can also provide comfort. Witness the feelings of well-being evoked by the mere mention of luxurious-sounding combinations: Smoked Salmon Canapés with Crème Fraîche and Caviar (page 11), Grilled Porterhouse Steak with Paprika-Parmesan Butter (page 45), Broiled Portobellos Topped with Creamy Scrambled Eggs (page 108),

Molten Chocolate Cakes with Cherries (page 194). But solace can come in more streamlined guises, too, including Tomato-Basil Soup (page 24), Fresh Tuna Tacos (page 87), Lighter Lasagna (page 120) and Cantaloupe Granita (page 215).

We can find inspiration in the creativity of cutting-edge American cooking: in Chicken and Kumquat Spring Rolls with Hoisin-Chili Sauce (page 15), Beef and Andouille Burgers with Asiago Cheese (page 44), Sea Bass with Moroccan Salsa (page 82), Shrimp with Spiced Masala and Coconut Milk (page 96) and Ginger Crème Brûlée (page 205). And we can be comforted by the realization that our cuisine is a beautiful blend of influences from other countries, as illustrated by Grilled

Shrimp with Spiced Masala and Coconut Milk (page 96)

Spiced Lamb Chops with Saffron Vegetables and Red Bell Pepper Sauce (page 50), French Bread with Kalamata Olives and Thyme (page 155), Gingerbread Squares with Honey-Mascarpone Cream (page 188) and Mango Cheesecake (page 192).

In short, whatever your personal taste in food, and however you define comfort, you'll find an abundance of excellent dishes in this latest collection of the most memorable recipes from the past year. We hope it will help to sustain and soothe you, your family, your friends . . . whomever you choose to share it with. What better reason could there be, then, to introduce our favorite recipes with a salute that always promises good eating and the nurturing warmth of friendship? *Bon Appétit!*

Smoky Black Bean Dip
(page 12)

Starters

Appetizers

Soups

Beverages

Steamed Clams with Ham, Bell Pepper and Basil

To keep clams alive until cooking and preserve freshness, make sure the shells are closed when purchased and store in the refrigerator in a bowl, not sealed in a plastic bag or submerged in water. Place a clean, damp cloth on top to avoid any cross-contamination of other food in the refrigerator.

6 tablespoons (¾ stick) butter
¾ cup diced smoked ham
¾ cup chopped red bell pepper
2 garlic cloves, minced
¼ teaspoon dried crushed red pepper

18 ½-inch-thick baguette slices
    Olive oil

5 pounds littleneck clams (35 to 40), scrubbed
1 cup Chardonnay
1 cup (loosely packed) chopped fresh basil

Melt butter in heavy medium skillet over low heat. Add ham and bell pepper and sauté until light brown, about 10 minutes. Add garlic and dried red pepper; stir 1 minute. Remove from heat.

Appetizers

Prepare barbecue (medium-high heat). Lightly brush baguette slices on both sides with oil. Grill bread until light brown on outside but soft on inside, about 2 minutes per side.

Combine clams and wine in large pot. Cover and boil over high heat until clams begin to open, about 8 minutes. Using slotted spoon, transfer clams to 6 bowls, discarding any clams that do not open. Add liquid in pot to skillet with ham-bell pepper mixture. Bring to boil over medium-high heat. Reduce heat to medium and simmer until liquid is slightly reduced, about 3 minutes. Remove from heat. Stir in basil. Pour mixture over clams, dividing equally. Serve clams, passing grilled bread separately.

6 SERVINGS

Smoked Salmon Canapés with Crème Fraîche and Caviar

12 (about) ¼-inch-thick slices challah bread
2 tablespoons (¼ stick) butter, melted
12 teaspoons crème fraîche* or sour cream
8 ounces thinly sliced smoked salmon
2 tablespoons (about) black caviar
24 dill sprigs

Preheat oven to 350°F. Using 1½-inch round cookie cutter, cut out 24 rounds from bread slices. Place bread rounds on baking sheet. Brush rounds with melted butter. Bake until golden, about 10 minutes. Cool. Spread ¼ teaspoon crème fraîche atop each bread round. Fold salmon slices decoratively atop crème fraîche. Top each with another ¼ teaspoon crème fraîche, then ¼ teaspoon caviar. Garnish each round with 1 dill sprig. (*Can be prepared 1 hour ahead. Chill.*)

*Crème fraîche is available in the dairy section of some specialty foods stores and some supermarkets nationwide.

8 SERVINGS

Well Bread

Exotic as the terms *canapés, fettunta, bruschetta* and *crostini* may sound, they all refer to simple slices of bread embellished with savory toppings.

Classic French canapés start with thinly sliced firm bread. Sometimes trimmed of the crust and cut into neat shapes, the plain or toasted slices are topped with seasoned butter, cheese or mayonnaise, often piped on in a decorative fashion. Garnishes such as seafood, meat, poultry or vegetables complete these formal-looking morsels.

In contrast, Italy's bread-based appetizers are rustic. Take fettunta, for example, which can be as simple as a thick slice of untoasted stale bread dipped into olive oil. The term *fettunta* is sometimes used interchangeably with *bruschetta,* which is a thick slice of bread that is grilled (*bruscare* means "to roast over coals"), then rubbed with garlic and drizzled with olive oil. Bruschetta is served with toppings like chopped tomatoes and basil or sautéed wild mushrooms.

Crostini are thinner slices of bread that are brushed with olive oil before being toasted in the oven. Chicken liver paté is the classic topping for crostini, but like bruschetta, crostini can be served with a variety of savory toppings.

Blue Cheese and Caramelized Shallot Dip

Blue Cheese and Caramelized Shallot Dip (pictured opposite) could be the ultimate, updated onion dip. Make it several hours in advance so that the flavors have a chance to blend. And as a general rule, allow ¼ cup to ⅓ cup dip per person.

1 tablespoon vegetable oil
1¼ cups thinly sliced shallots (about 4 ounces)
¾ cup mayonnaise
¾ cup sour cream
4 ounces blue cheese, room temperature

Heat oil in medium saucepan over medium-low heat. Add shallots. Cover; cook until shallots are brown, stirring often, about 20 minutes. Cool.

Whisk mayonnaise and sour cream in medium bowl. Add cheese. Using rubber spatula, mash mixture until smooth. Stir in shallots. Season dip to taste with salt and pepper. Cover dip and chill until flavors blend, about 2 hours. (*Can be prepared 2 days ahead. Keep refrigerated.*) Serve dip chilled.

MAKES ABOUT 2 CUPS

Smoky Black Bean Dip

4 bacon slices
1 medium onion, chopped
1 small red bell pepper, seeded, chopped
½ teaspoon ground cumin
½ teaspoon dried oregano
2 15-ounce cans black beans, undrained
1 teaspoon chopped seeded canned chipotle chilies*
½ cup sour cream
2 tablespoons chopped fresh cilantro

Cook bacon in large skillet over medium heat until crisp, 6 minutes. Drain and coarsely chop. Pour off all but 1 tablespoon drippings from skillet. Add onion and bell pepper; sauté until onion is soft, 6 minutes. Add cumin and oregano; sauté 1 minute. Add beans with their liquid and chipotles. Simmer over medium-low heat until slightly thickened, stirring occasionally, 5 minutes.

Transfer 1 cup bean mixture to processor. Blend until smooth. Stir into remaining bean mixture. Season to taste. Transfer to bowl. Cover and chill 2 hours. (*Can be prepared 2 days ahead. Chill dip and bacon separately.*)

Stir half of bacon into dip. Top with sour cream. Sprinkle with cilantro and remaining bacon. Serve dip chilled or at room temperature.

*Chipotle chilies canned in a spicy tomato sauce, sometimes called adobo, *are available at Latin American markets, specialty foods stores and some supermarkets.*

MAKES ABOUT 4 CUPS

Pear, Onion and Dry Jack Cheese Strudels

These delicious strudels can be put together one day before baking. Try garnishing with thin slices of apple that have been soaked for a few minutes in two cups of water spiked with the juice of one lemon. The lemon will keep the apple from turning brown.

6	tablespoons (¾ stick) unsalted butter
1	onion, chopped
1	Bosc pear, peeled, halved, cored, sliced
¾	cup (packed) grated dry Jack cheese or ½ cup grated Parmesan cheese and ¼ cup grated sharp white cheddar cheese
3	teaspoons whole grain Dijon mustard
½	teaspoon salt
4	sheets frozen phyllo pastry, thawed

Melt 2 tablespoons butter in heavy medium skillet over medium heat. Add onion and sauté until brown, about 7 minutes. Add pear and sauté 3 minutes. Transfer pear mixture to medium bowl. Cool slightly. Stir in dry Jack cheese, mustard and salt.

Melt remaining 4 tablespoons butter in small saucepan over medium heat. Place 1 phyllo sheet on work surface. (Cover remaining phyllo with plastic wrap and damp kitchen towel.) Brush with melted butter. Top with second phyllo sheet. Brush with melted butter. Arrange half of pear mixture in log along 1 short end of phyllo, leaving 1-inch border at each end of pear mixture. Fold in sides and roll up tightly into log. Brush all over with butter. Transfer to large baking sheet. Repeat with remaining phyllo, butter and pear mixture. (*Strudels can be prepared 1 day ahead. Cover and refrigerate.*)

Preheat oven to 375°F. Bake strudels until golden brown, about 18 minutes. Cool 5 minutes. Transfer 1 strudel to cutting board. Cut on diagonal into 12 pieces. Repeat with remaining strudel. Transfer to platter and serve.

MAKES ABOUT 24 PIECES

Crab Cakes with Green Onion and Dill

3	cups fresh breadcrumbs made from crustless French bread
8	ounces crabmeat, well drained
1	green onion, chopped
2	tablespoons chopped fresh dill
1¼	teaspoons Old Bay seasoning
3	tablespoons mayonnaise
1	teaspoon Dijon mustard
1	teaspoon fresh lemon juice
1	large egg, beaten to blend
3	tablespoons butter

Mix 2 cups breadcrumbs, crabmeat, onion, dill and Old Bay seasoning in large bowl until combined. Stir in mayonnaise, mustard and lemon juice. Season with salt and pepper. Stir in egg. Form mixture into eight 1/2-inch-thick patties. Place 1 cup breadcrumbs on plate; coat cakes with crumbs. Transfer to baking sheet. Chill at least 30 minutes and up to 4 hours.

Melt butter in heavy large skillet over medium heat. In 2 batches, sauté cakes until golden, about 3 minutes per side. Serve hot.

8 SERVINGS

Chicken and Kumquat Spring Rolls with Hoisin-Chili Sauce

1	tablespoon oriental sesame oil
8	ounces chicken thigh meat, cut into 1x1/4-inch strips
1/2	red onion, chopped
2	ounces kumquats in syrup* (about 4), drained, thinly sliced
6	ounces mung bean sprouts
1/4	cup chopped fresh basil
1/4	cup chopped fresh mint
16	rice paper rounds (about 1/2 package)
8	large whole iceberg lettuce leaves
1	8-ounce bottle hoisin sauce*
2	teaspoons chili-garlic paste*

Heat sesame oil in heavy large skillet over medium-high heat. Sprinkle chicken with salt and pepper. Add chicken and onion to skillet and sauté 3 minutes. Stir in kumquats. Remove from heat. Cool. Stir in bean sprouts.

Toss basil and mint in small bowl. Dip 1 rice paper round into bowl of warm water until soft, about 10 seconds. Place on moist kitchen towel to drain 1 minute. Repeat with another rice paper round; place second round atop first for double thickness. Top with 1 lettuce leaf, then place 1/8 of chicken mixture near bottom edge of round. Sprinkle with 1/8 of herb mixture. Fold in sides of round, then roll up, starting near filling. Repeat with remaining rounds, lettuce leaves, chicken mixture and herb mixture.

Whisk hoisin sauce and chili-garlic paste in medium bowl to blend. Slice each roll diagonally into 4 pieces, for total of 32 pieces. Pour sauce into individual shallow bowls and place in center of each of 8 plates; surround with spring rolls and serve.

Available at Asian markets, specialty foods stores and some supermarkets.

8 SERVINGS

Crumbs Fraîches

In many *Bon Appétit* recipes, we call for fresh breadcrumbs, which lend a different texture and flavor to dishes than commercially available counterparts do. In seconds, a food processor can turn fresh bread into breadcrumbs, ready to coat baked, broiled or fried foods or to add body to stuffings, fillings or meat loaves.

Start with a loaf of French or sourdough bread that has a dense, firm crumb; day-old bread, which is slightly less moist, will process to a more uniform consistency, though you can also use fresh bread. Cut the bread into slices of equal thickness and trim off the crusts, which will interfere with uniform processing and can also spoil the even color sometimes wanted for crumbs. Tear the slices into uniform chunks and drop them into a processor fitted with the metal blade. Using on/off turns, process until the bread forms crumbs of the desired consistency.

Fresh breadcrumbs will keep in the refrigerator for up to four days or in the freezer for up to a year if they are securely sealed in an airtight container.

Pita Toasts with Wild Mushroom Sauté

 3 pita breads, each cut horizontally in half, each half cut into 6 wedges
 5 tablespoons olive oil
 3 tablespoons butter
 ½ cup minced shallots (about 1¾ ounces)
 2 garlic cloves, minced
 2 pounds wild mushrooms (crimini, oyster and stemmed shiitake), sliced
 2 teaspoons minced fresh thyme
 ½ cup dry white wine
 ½ cup whipping cream
 4 tablespoons minced fresh chives

Preheat oven to 350°F. Place pita wedges on 2 baking sheets. Brush with 3 tablespoons oil. Sprinkle with salt and pepper. Bake until crisp, about 12 minutes. Cool. *(Can be made 1 day ahead. Store airtight at room temperature.)*

Melt butter with remaining olive oil in large skillet over medium-high heat. Add shallots and garlic; sauté 2 minutes. Add mushrooms and 1 teaspoon thyme; sauté until golden brown, about 15 minutes. Add wine and boil until liquid evaporates, 2 minutes. Mix in cream, 2 tablespoons chives and remaining thyme. Simmer until cream thickens, 1 minute. Season to taste.

Sprinkle with remaining 2 tablespoons chives. Spoon onto toasts.

10 SERVINGS

The Pita Toasts with Wild Mushroom Sauté (pictured opposite) can easily be prepared in half an hour. To save time and allow them to cool, bake the toasts a day ahead of time and store them in an airtight container at room temperature.

Warm Olives with Fennel and Orange

 1½ cups assorted brine-cured olives
 2 cups water
 2 teaspoons extra-virgin olive oil
 ½ teaspoon chopped fresh thyme
 1 garlic clove, minced
 ¼ teaspoon fennel seeds, ground
 ¼ teaspoon grated orange peel
 ½ teaspoon white wine vinegar

Place olives in medium bowl with 2 cups water; let stand 10 minutes. Drain. Combine olives, oil, thyme, garlic, fennel seeds and orange peel in small skillet. Cook over medium-high heat until garlic is fragrant and oil is hot, about 5 minutes. Remove from heat. Stir in vinegar. Cool slightly; serve warm.

6 SERVINGS

Gift Wraps

Call them wrappers or skins: Anyone who has eaten in a Chinese restaurant knows the thin, edible noodles that encase wontons, egg rolls, potstickers and other dumplings. Most are made from a dough of wheat flour, eggs and water.

Packages of these wrappers can be found in refrigerator or freezer cases of Asian markets and well-stocked grocery stores. They may be stored in airtight containers in the refrigerator for up to a week or in the freezer for up to two months.

Wrappers vary in the thickness, size and shape in which they are cut, but are often interchangeable. Egg roll and wonton wrappers are generally thin, and the former (usually six- to seven-inch squares) can be cut into quarters to make wonton wrappers. Potsticker wrappers are thicker circles of about three inches in diameter, but wonton or egg roll wrappers trimmed to the appropriate size and shape may be substituted. Slightly thicker Japanese *gyoza* wrappers may also be used.

Since their ingredients are the same as those used in most European noodle doughs, these wrappers possess a versatility that extends well beyond Asian kitchens. Whether used to make snacks such as Latin-style empanadas (at right) or the Jewish meat-filled soup dumplings known as kreplach, they produce excellent results.

Quick Chicken and Olive Empanadas

    8 ounces skinless boneless chicken breast halves, cut into ½-inch cubes
    ¼ cup chopped onion
    ¼ cup chopped red bell pepper
    ¼ cup chopped tomato
    ¼ cup water
    2 tablespoons raisins
    2 tablespoons chopped fresh parsley
    1 tablespoon tomato paste
    1 tablespoon chopped pimiento-stuffed green olives
    1 garlic clove, minced
    ½ teaspoon ground cumin
    2 tablespoons dry breadcrumbs

   36 gyoza (potsticker) wrappers*
    1 large egg, lightly beaten

    2 cups (about) canola oil

Combine first 11 ingredients in heavy medium skillet. Cook over medium-high heat until chicken is cooked through, stirring occasionally, about 5 minutes. Transfer mixture to processor; grind coarsely. Transfer to medium bowl. Mix in breadcrumbs. Season filling to taste with salt and pepper.

Refrigerate filling until cold, about 1 hour. (*Can be prepared 1 day ahead. Cover and keep refrigerated.*)

Line baking sheet with foil; sprinkle with flour. Place gyoza wrappers on work surface. Lightly brush edge of each wrapper with beaten egg. Place heaping 1 teaspoon filling in center of each gyoza wrapper. Fold gyoza wrapper in half and crimp edges with tines of fork to seal. Transfer empanadas to prepared baking sheet. (*Can be prepared 6 hours ahead. Cover empanadas and refrigerate.*)

Heat canola oil in heavy medium skillet over medium-high heat. Working in batches, add empanadas to oil and fry until golden brown, about 30 seconds per side. Drain empanadas on paper towels. Serve warm.

Can be found at Asian markets and in the refrigerator section of many supermarkets. Or substitute wonton wrappers cut into thirty-six 3^1/$_2$-inch rounds.

MAKES 36

Pastry-wrapped Brie with Raspberries

½ cup raspberry preserves
¼ cup fresh or frozen unsweetened raspberries, thawed
½ teaspoon finely chopped fresh rosemary leaves
 1 sheet frozen puff pastry (half of 17.3-ounce package), thawed
 1 13.2-ounce Baby Brie cheese (about 6 to 7 inches in diameter)
 1 large egg, beaten to blend (for glaze)

   Crackers and baguette slices
   Grapes

Keeping frozen puff pastry on hand can save time in the preparation of appetizers and desserts.

Preheat oven to 400°F. Stir preserves, berries and rosemary in small bowl to blend. Season berry mixture with pepper. Roll out pastry on lightly floured surface to 12-inch square. Cut top rind off cheese; discard rind. Place cheese, rindless side up, in center of pastry. Spoon raspberry mixture atop cheese. Fold pastry on 2 opposite sides over cheese. Brush remaining 2 sides of pastry with glaze. Fold over cheese; press seams to seal. Brush pastry with glaze; place on baking sheet.

Bake cheese until pastry is deep golden brown (top of pastry may split open), about 30 minutes. Let cool 20 minutes. Place baked cheese on serving platter. Surround with crackers, baguette slices and grapes.

8 SERVINGS

Double-Salmon Dip

To create a smooth, light texture for the Double-Salmon
Dip (pictured opposite), avoid
cream cheese sold in blocks;
instead, use the whipped
cream cheese sold in tubs.

2 8-ounce containers whipped cream cheese
3 tablespoons whole milk
4 ounces thinly sliced smoked salmon, cut into ½-inch pieces
2 tablespoons chopped fresh chives
1 2-ounce jar red salmon caviar

Mash whipped cream cheese and milk in medium bowl. Fold in salmon and 1 tablespoon chives. Season with pepper to taste. Gently fold in caviar. Cover and chill 2 hours to blend flavors. *(Can be prepared 1 day ahead. Keep chilled.)* Sprinkle dip with remaining 1 tablespoon chives. Serve dip chilled.

MAKES ABOUT 3 CUPS

Beef Cubes with Red Bell Peppers and Cilantro Sauce

2 cups (packed) stemmed fresh cilantro (2 to 3 large bunches)
½ cup olive oil
3 tablespoons fresh lime juice
1 tablespoon chopped jalapeño chili
1½ teaspoons dried oregano
1 large garlic clove, chopped
¼ cup coarsely chopped red onion
4 pounds beef tenderloin, cut into 1-inch cubes (about 48 cubes)
2 large red bell peppers, halved, seeded, cut into 1-inch squares
  Olive oil

Puree first 6 ingredients in processor until almost smooth. Add red onion and process until finely chopped but not ground. Season cilantro sauce generously with salt and pepper. *(Sauce can be prepared up to 1 day ahead. Transfer to small bowl; cover and refrigerate.)*

Preheat broiler. Place beef and red bell peppers in separate bowls. Mix enough oil into beef and into bell peppers to coat. Spread out beef on large baking sheet; sprinkle with salt and pepper. Spread out peppers on another large baking sheet; sprinkle with salt and pepper. Broil beef to desired doneness, about 3 minutes per side for medium-rare. Broil peppers until just tender and beginning to brown, about 3 minutes. Skewer 1 beef cube and 1 pepper square with toothpick. Repeat with remaining beef and pepper. Arrange on platter and serve with cilantro sauce.

MAKES ABOUT 48

Grape Leaves Stuffed with Rice, Dill and Walnuts

1 16-ounce jar grape leaves
8 cups water
1 pound long-grain white rice
2 teaspoons salt

1 cup olive oil
1½ pounds onions, chopped (about 4⅓ cups)
4 large garlic cloves, minced
1 cup chopped fresh parsley
¾ cup finely chopped walnuts
¾ cup chopped fresh dill
1 teaspoon ground black pepper
2 cups crumbled feta cheese (about 8 ounces)

½ cup fresh lemon juice
  Lemon wedges

Grape leaves, invaluable in Mediterranean cuisine, are available at Greek, Middle Eastern and most Italian markets. They lend an exotic touch to this delicious do-ahead appetizer.

Cover grape leaves in large bowl with water. Let soak while preparing rice filling, separating leaves occasionally. Bring 4 cups water, rice and 1 teaspoon salt to boil in heavy saucepan over high heat. Reduce heat, cover and cook until rice is tender and water is absorbed, 20 minutes. Uncover; set aside.

Heat ½ cup oil in heavy large pot over medium heat. Add onions and sauté until beginning to turn golden, about 15 minutes. Add garlic; sauté 1 minute. Remove from heat. Stir in parsley, walnuts, dill, pepper and remaining 1 teaspoon salt. Cool slightly. Mix in cheese, then rice. Cool completely.

Preheat oven to 375°F. Place 1 large grape leaf, vein side up, on work surface. Cut off stem. Patch with pieces of other leaves if needed to form about 5- to 6-inch surface area. Spoon scant ¼ cup filling in center of leaf. Fold bottom of leaf over filling. Fold in sides. Roll up to enclose filling in leaf. Arrange seam side down on baking sheet. Repeat to use up remaining filling.

Line bottom of two 13x9x2-inch glass baking dishes with any remaining grape leaves. Divide stuffed grape leaves between prepared dishes, arranging seam side down in rows in single layer.

Mix remaining 4 cups water, ½ cup oil and lemon juice in medium bowl to blend. Pour enough lemon-oil mixture over stuffed grape leaves in each dish to cover. Cover dishes with foil. Bake until mixture is absorbed and flavors blend, about 1 hour. Uncover; cool to room temperature. *(Can be prepared 4 days ahead. Cover and refrigerate. Let stand at room temperature 1 hour before serving.)* Arrange stuffed leaves on plates. Garnish with lemon wedges.

MAKES ABOUT 55

Smoked Fish Chowder

This quick recipe (pictured opposite) doubles or triples easily to serve four or six people with bread and salad as a light dinner or lunch.

1 tablespoon butter
2 cups chopped onions
1 8-ounce bottle clam juice
8 ounces red-skinned potatoes, sliced into ¼-inch-thick rounds
1 tablespoon chopped fresh thyme
2 cups half and half
1 4.5-ounce package smoked trout, torn into small pieces

Melt butter in heavy medium saucepan over medium heat. Add onions; sauté until soft, about 5 minutes. Add clam juice, potatoes and thyme. Cover and simmer until potatoes are tender, stirring occasionally, about 10 minutes. Add half and half and trout. Simmer 10 minutes. Season to taste with salt and pepper and serve.

2 SERVINGS

Tomato-Basil Soup

3 tablespoons extra-virgin olive oil
2 cups chopped onions
1 large russet potato (about 14 ounces), peeled, cut into 1-inch pieces
2 pounds plum tomatoes, seeded, cut into 1-inch pieces (about 6 cups)
3 cups (or more) water
1 cup (loosely packed) fresh basil leaves plus 4 teaspoons chopped fresh basil

Heat oil in heavy large pot over medium heat. Add onions and sauté until golden, about 15 minutes. Add potato and sauté until light brown, about 10 minutes. Add tomatoes and stir until juices form, about 5 minutes. Add 3 cups water; bring to boil. Reduce heat to low, cover and simmer until potato is tender, about 25 minutes.

Working in batches, puree soup in blender until smooth. Return soup to pot. Thin with additional water, if desired. Stir in 1 cup basil leaves. Simmer uncovered 5 minutes. Season soup to taste with salt and pepper. Ladle soup into 4 bowls. Sprinkle each with 1 teaspoon chopped basil.

4 SERVINGS

Soups

Chilled Cream of Zucchini Soup
with Mussels and Fresh Mint

When making this delicious soup, take care to use only mussels that open during cooking. Discard mussels that remain closed.

5	tablespoons olive oil
1	large onion, chopped
1	large carrot, chopped
3	garlic cloves, minced
3	fresh thyme sprigs
4	cups chicken stock or canned low-salt chicken broth
2	cups dry white wine
2¼	pounds fresh mussels, scrubbed, debearded
2¼	pounds zucchini, trimmed, cut into ½-inch pieces (about 7 cups)
½	cup whipping cream
¼	cup chopped fresh mint

Heat 2 tablespoons oil in heavy large pot over medium heat. Add onion, carrot, garlic and thyme; sauté until vegetables are tender, stirring occasionally, about 10 minutes. Add stock and wine; bring to boil. Add mussels; cover and cook until mussels open, about 5 minutes (discard any mussels that do not open). Using slotted spoon, transfer mussels to large bowl; cool slightly. Remove mussels from shells; cover and refrigerate until ready to use. Strain stock mixture and any accumulated mussel liquid into medium bowl; discard vegetables.

Heat 3 tablespoons oil in large skillet over medium heat. Add zucchini; sauté until tender but not brown, about 20 minutes. Add 2½ cups strained stock. Bring to boil. Cool slightly. Puree soup in batches in blender until smooth. Transfer to large saucepan; mix in cream. Thin with more strained stock, if desired. Reserve any remaining stock for another use. Season with salt and pepper. Refrigerate until cold, about 4 hours. *(Soup and mussels can be made 6 hours ahead. Cover separately; keep chilled.)*

Divide zucchini soup among 6 bowls. Top each with mussels, dividing equally. Sprinkle with chopped mint.

6 SERVINGS

Gingered Parsnip Bisque

3	tablespoons butter
2½	cups chopped leeks (about 2 large; white and pale green parts only)
½	cup chopped celery
3	tablespoons minced peeled fresh ginger
2	large shallots, minced
⅛	teaspoon cayenne pepper
4½	cups canned low-salt chicken broth
1½	pounds parsnips, peeled, coarsely chopped (about 4 cups)
2	cups half and half

Melt butter in heavy large pot over medium heat. Add next 5 ingredients and sauté until vegetables are tender, about 5 minutes. Stir in broth and parsnips; bring to boil. Reduce heat to medium-low and simmer until parsnips are tender, about 20 minutes. Cool slightly.

Working in batches, puree soup in blender until smooth. Strain into another large pot; discard solids in strainer. Whisk in half and half. Simmer soup over medium heat until heated through, about 10 minutes. Season soup with salt and pepper.

6 TO 8 SERVINGS

Ginger in a Snap

A signature Asian seasoning, ginger is celebrated in many cuisines for its distinctive flavor: refreshing, slightly sweet and spicy-hot. These qualities can be imparted to a wide range of recipes by using ginger in one of its various commercially available forms.

- **Fresh Ginger:** Tan-skinned pieces of the knobby underground stem are found in produce sections, ready to be peeled and then sliced, chopped, grated or shredded to flavor stir-fries, soups, stews and steamed dishes.

- **Crystallized Ginger:** Pieces of tender young ginger are cooked in sugar syrup, then coated with granulated sugar. Use these in candies, desserts or baked goods, or nibble with tea.

- **Pickled Ginger:** A popular condiment for sushi or garnish for other seafood, poultry, meat, rice or noodle dishes, this is made by slicing peeled ginger thinly and preserving it with rice vinegar, rice wine or brine.

- **Ground Ginger:** Commonly found in the spice section, this dried, ground form is used in cakes, cookies and breads.

Turkey-Sage Chowder

4 bacon slices (about 4 ounces), coarsely chopped
2 cups chopped onions
1 pound russet potatoes, peeled, cut into ½-inch pieces
2 cups whole milk
1 cup canned low-salt chicken broth
⅔ cup condensed cream of potato soup (from one 10¾-ounce can)
2 tablespoons chopped fresh sage
2½ cups diced cooked turkey

Cook bacon in heavy large saucepan over medium heat until crisp, about 8 minutes. Transfer bacon to paper towels to drain. Pour off all but 2 tablespoons drippings from pan. Increase heat to medium-high; add onions and sauté until tender, about 5 minutes. Mix in potatoes, milk, broth, cream of potato soup and 1 tablespoon sage. Bring to boil. Reduce heat to medium-

low and simmer until potatoes are tender, stirring occasionally, about 10 minutes. Add turkey meat, bacon and remaining 1 tablespoon sage. Simmer soup until heated through, stirring occasionally, about 4 minutes. Season to taste with salt and pepper and serve.

6 TO 8 SERVINGS

Chilled Avocado-Lime Soup

This soup makes a wonderful picnic starter, transported in a thermos with the garnishes kept separate until it is served.

2 tablespoons (¼ stick) butter
3 shallots, minced (about ½ cup)
1 tablespoon minced peeled fresh ginger
2 14½-ounce cans low-salt chicken broth
2 tablespoons fresh lime juice
¼ teaspoon cayenne pepper
2 13-ounce avocados, halved, pitted, peeled, mashed (about 2¼ cups)
½ cup half and half
   Chopped fresh cilantro
   Lime slices (optional)

Melt butter in medium saucepan over medium heat. Add shallots and ginger; sauté 1 minute. Add chicken broth, lime juice and cayenne pepper; bring to boil. Reduce heat to medium-low and simmer 3 minutes. Transfer mixture to large bowl. Puree avocados and half and half in blender. Whisk into soup. Season with salt and pepper. Cover and refrigerate until cold, at least 3 hours and up to 1 day. Ladle avocado-lime soup into bowls; garnish with cilantro and with lime slices, if desired.

6 TO 8 SERVINGS

Very Simple Pumpkin Soup

> 2 15-ounce cans pure pumpkin
> 4 cups water
> 1 cup half and half
> 1 garlic clove, pressed
> ¼ cup pure maple syrup
> 4 tablespoons unsalted butter
> ½ teaspoon Chinese five-spice powder*
>
> 4 ounces fresh shiitake mushrooms, stemmed, sliced

Bring first 4 ingredients to simmer in large saucepan over medium-high heat, whisking often. Whisk in syrup, 2 tablespoons butter and five-spice powder. Simmer soup 10 minutes, whisking often. Season with salt and pepper. *(Soup can be prepared 1 day ahead. Chill until cold, then cover and keep chilled. Bring to simmer before serving.)*

Melt remaining 2 tablespoons butter in heavy medium skillet over medium-high heat. Add mushrooms; sauté until tender, about 10 minutes. Divide soup among 6 bowls. Sprinkle soup with mushroom slices, dividing equally; serve.

A blend of ground anise, cinnamon, star anise, cloves and ginger, available in the spice section of most supermarkets.

6 SERVINGS

**Casual Supper
for Six**

Very Simple Pumpkin Soup
(at left)

Rustic Bread

**Spice-rubbed Butterflied
Leg of Lamb**
(page 57)

Lemon-Sage Green Beans
(page 133)

Syrah

Bakery Lime Pie

Fish Soup with Aioli Croutons

The garlic-infused condiment known as aioli, made for this authentic French bistro dish, is also delicious with either grilled seafood or poultry.

¾ cup mayonnaise
2 teaspoons Dijon mustard
2 teaspoons red wine vinegar
2 garlic cloves, minced
¾ teaspoon hot pepper sauce
6 tablespoons olive oil

4 leeks (white and pale green parts only), sliced
2 carrots, cut into ½-inch pieces
1 fennel bulb, cut into ½-inch pieces
2 shallots, chopped
6 large garlic cloves, chopped
2 plum tomatoes, coarsely chopped
2 tablespoons tomato paste
½ teaspoon dried thyme
¼ teaspoon saffron threads
1½ cups dry white wine
5 cups (or more) chicken stock or canned low-salt chicken broth
3 pounds assorted fish fillets (such as sea bass, snapper and orange roughy), cut into 2-inch pieces

1 French bread baguette, cut into ⅓-inch-thick slices, toasted
Chopped fresh parsley

Whisk first 5 ingredients and 3 tablespoons oil in small bowl to blend. Season aioli to taste with salt and pepper. (*Aioli can be prepared 1 day ahead. Cover and refrigerate.*)

Heat remaining 3 tablespoons oil in heavy large pot over medium heat. Add leeks, carrots, fennel and shallots; sauté until golden brown, about 15 minutes. Add garlic and sauté 2 minutes. Mix in tomatoes, tomato paste, thyme and saffron. Add wine and boil 5 minutes. Add 5 cups stock and bring to boil. Reduce heat and simmer 15 minutes to blend flavors. Add fish and simmer until fish is cooked through, about 5 minutes. Cool slightly.

Working in batches, puree soup in blender. Working in batches, strain soup through coarse sieve set over large bowl, pressing firmly to force as much of solids as possible through sieve. Return soup to pot. Season with salt and pepper. *(Can be prepared 1 day ahead. Cover and chill.)*

Spread enough aioli over each toast to cover. Bring soup to simmer, thinning with more stock if desired. Ladle soup into bowls. Top each with 2 toasts. Sprinkle with parsley and serve.

6 TO 8 SERVINGS

Cream of Mushroom Soup

2 tablespoons (¼ stick) butter

3 leeks, halved, thinly sliced (white and pale green parts only)

2 pounds button mushrooms, sliced

2 garlic cloves, minced

¼ cup long-grain white rice

3¼ cups (or more) canned low-salt chicken broth

3¼ cups canned beef broth

½ cup whipping cream

¼ cup chopped fresh chives

Melt butter in heavy large pot over medium heat. Add leeks and sauté until tender, about 5 minutes. Increase heat to medium-high. Add mushrooms and sauté until mushrooms are soft and dry, about 10 minutes. Add garlic; sauté 1 minute. Stir in rice. Add 3¼ cups chicken broth and beef broth to pot. Bring to boil. Reduce heat to low, cover and simmer until rice is very tender, about 30 minutes. Cool slightly. Working in batches, puree soup in blender until smooth. Return soup to pot. Stir in cream. Thin with more chicken broth, if desired. *(Soup can be prepared 1 day ahead. Cool slightly, then cover and refrigerate. Bring to simmer before continuing.)*

Ladle soup into 8 bowls. Sprinkle with chives and serve.

8 SERVINGS

Traditional cream of mushroom soup gets a flavor boost from leeks and beef broth. Chopped fresh chives are a colorful garnish.

Tropical Margarita

Mixed drinks are back big time, and they're being updated and transformed into great new cocktails. Among them (pictured opposite, from left): Tropical Margarita, Lemon-Cassis Martini and Gingered Gin and Tonic.

9 tablespoons frozen guava-passion-orange concentrate, thawed
½ cup tequila
4 teaspoons frozen limeade, thawed
4 teaspoons fresh lime juice
16 ice cubes, coarsely cracked
Fresh lime slices (optional)
Orange peel twists (optional)

Mix first 4 ingredients in glass measuring cup. Fill 2 Margarita glasses with ice. Pour Margarita mixture over. Garnish with lime slices and orange peel twists, if desired, and serve.

2 SERVINGS

Gingered Gin and Tonic

1 cup water
¾ cup sugar
2 tablespoons finely grated peeled fresh ginger

2 cups tonic water
1 cup gin
¼ cup fresh lime juice
24 ice cubes
Fresh ginger slices (optional)
Lime wedges (optional)

Combine 1 cup water, sugar and ginger in heavy small saucepan over medium heat. Stir until sugar dissolves. Increase heat and boil until reduced to 1⅓ cups, about 3 minutes. Cool syrup, then strain. (*Can be prepared 1 week ahead. Cover and refrigerate.*)

Mix tonic water, gin, lime juice and ½ cup ginger syrup in glass measuring cup. Taste, adding more syrup if desired (reserve remaining syrup for another use). Divide ice among 4 tall glasses. Pour gin and tonic mixture over. Garnish with fresh ginger slices and lime wedges, if desired.

4 SERVINGS

Beverages

Lemon-Cassis Martini

¾ cup vodka
4 teaspoons fresh lemon juice
2 teaspoons sugar
½ teaspoon grated lemon peel
1 tablespoon crème de cassis
Ice cubes
Lemon peel twists

Mix first 4 ingredients in glass measuring cup. Let stand 10 minutes. Strain into Martini shaker or another cup. Mix in cassis. Add ice; shake or stir until very cold. Strain into glasses. Garnish with lemon peel twists.

2 SERVINGS

"One is alright, two is too many, and three is not enough," quipped James Thurber of the Martini. Indeed, that observation seems even truer today in light of the ongoing Martini renaissance, which has produced a wide range of tempting cocktails sharing the name.

Classically, the drink is made by shaking or stirring gin and a hint of dry vermouth with ice, and serving it in a well-iced Martini glass with a green olive garnish. Custom aside, many aficionados long ago replaced the gin with premium vodka.

But that simple substitution doesn't begin to suggest the variations concocted today from flavored spirits and all manner of liqueurs and other flourishes. Consider the Cajun Martini, made with pepper vodka, vermouth and a jalapeño chili garnish; the Banana Rum Martini, a blend of dark rum and crème de bananes; the Chocolate Martini, which combines plain vodka and white crème de cacao; or James Bond's favorite, the Vesper: three parts gin and one part vodka, a splash of Lillet and a slice of lemon.

Faced with such a bill of fare, who, indeed, could stop at one?

Honeyed Lemonade

When making fresh lemonade, always start with room-temperature lemons. Using the palm of your hand, press down firmly on each lemon as you roll it back and forth on the kitchen counter. This will break open the juice sacs.

3 cups water
½ cup honey
½ cup sugar
¼ cup minced peeled fresh ginger
1¼ cups fresh lemon juice
  Ice cubes

Bring 1 cup water, honey, sugar and ginger to boil in heavy medium saucepan over high heat, stirring until sugar dissolves. Boil 5 minutes. Remove from heat and cool. Strain syrup into pitcher. Mix in lemon juice and remaining 2 cups water. Fill pitcher with ice. Let stand 5 minutes. Fill 4 to 6 tall glasses with ice; add lemonade.

4 TO 6 SERVINGS

Raspberry Lemonade

1	10-ounce package frozen raspberries in syrup, thawed
1¼	cups fresh lemon juice
¾	cup sugar
2	cups water
	Ice cubes
	Lemon slices (optional)
	Fresh raspberries (optional)

Puree thawed berries in processor. Strain into pitcher, pressing on solids in strainer to extract as much liquid as possible. Mix in lemon juice and sugar; stir until sugar dissolves. Mix in 2 cups water. Fill pitcher with ice. Let stand 5 minutes. Fill 4 to 6 tall glasses with ice; add lemonade. Garnish with lemon slices and fresh raspberries, if desired.

4 TO 6 SERVINGS

Crushed-Mint Lemonade

6	large lemons, scrubbed, thinly sliced
1	small bunch fresh mint, thick stems trimmed (about 2 loosely packed cups)
1¼	cups sugar
½	cup fresh lemon juice
2	cups water
	Ice cubes

Using potato masher, mash sliced lemons, mint, 1 cup sugar and lemon juice in large bowl until juicy, about 5 minutes. Strain lemon mixture through coarse sieve set over another large bowl, pressing masher on solids in sieve to extract some pulp and as much liquid as possible. Mix 2 cups water and remaining ¼ cup sugar into lemon liquid and pulp in bowl. Fill pitcher with ice; pour lemonade over ice. Let stand 5 minutes. Fill 4 to 6 tall glasses with ice; add lemonade.

4 TO 6 SERVINGS

When it's time to fire up the grill, this is a terrific thirst-quencher for guests and cook alike. To transform it into a cocktail, just add a splash of lemon vodka.

Flying South

Distill the essence of southern hospitality down to beverage form and you find the mint julep, official drink of the Kentucky Derby.

The cocktail's basic elements are simple: sugar water, bourbon, fresh mint and crushed ice. Yet controversy swirls around the fine details, particularly the mint. Purists hold that it enters the drink only at the end of mixing, in the form of a sprig garnish, ready to scent each sip. However, those who prefer a more prominent mint flavor may steep the herb in the sugar water; or, more commonly, might crush or "muddle" some mint with water at the bottom of each glass before adding ice and bourbon.

Whatever the approach, almost everyone agrees that there's only one kind of container in which to serve a julep: a straight-sided tumbler made of silver or pewter. The metal readily conducts cold from the ice, causing condensation on the outside and making the julep all the more refreshing on a sultry southern day.

Mint Julep Spritzer

    ¾ cup fresh lemon juice
    ⅔ cup sugar
    1 cup (packed) fresh mint leaves, plus 8 fresh mint sprigs
    1 cup bourbon
    2 10-ounce bottles of chilled club soda
    6 cups crushed ice

Mix fresh lemon juice, sugar and fresh mint leaves in small bowl until sugar dissolves; press on mint with back of spoon to crush lightly. Let stand 30 minutes. Strain mint-lemon mixture into pitcher. Add bourbon, then club soda and ice. Pour into 8 glasses. Garnish each with mint sprig.

    8 SERVINGS

Mojito

    3 cups (packed) fresh mint leaves
    9 tablespoons sugar
 1½ cups light rum
    ½ cup fresh lime juice
    6 cups club soda
    6 cups crushed ice
    6 lime wedges

Reserve 6 mint leaves. Place remaining leaves in bowl. Add sugar. Mash until mint is aromatic and oils are released. Add rum and lime juice; stir until sugar dissolves. Strain into pitcher. (Can be prepared 2 hours ahead; chill.)

Add club soda; stir gently. Fill each of 6 glasses with 1 cup crushed ice. Pour mojito over and garnish each glass with 1 mint leaf and 1 lime wedge.

    6 SERVINGS

Apricot Bellini

    1 750-ml bottle of chilled brut Champagne
 2½ cups chilled apricot nectar
    3 tablespoons Grand Marnier or other orange liqueur

Mix chilled Champagne, chilled apricot nectar and Grand Marnier in tall pitcher. Pour into Champagne flutes and serve.

    6 TO 8 SERVINGS

White Zinfandel Sangria

1 750-ml bottle of chilled white Zinfandel

½ cup peach schnapps

2 tablespoons Cointreau or other orange liqueur

2 tablespoons sugar

2 cinnamon sticks, broken in half

1 lemon, sliced

1 orange, sliced

1 peach, sliced into wedges

1 10-ounce bottle of chilled club soda

Ice cubes

A new take on an old favorite, this drink complements many Latin foods—even simple tortilla chips.

Mix first 8 ingredients in tall pitcher. Refrigerate at least 30 minutes to allow flavors to blend. Mix in club soda. Fill 6 wineglasses with ice cubes. Pour sangria over ice and serve.

6 SERVINGS

Roast Chicken with Herb Butter, Onions and Garlic
(page 70)

Main Courses

Meats

Poultry

Seafood

Meatless

Pasta & Pizza

Braised Meatballs in Red-Wine Gravy

This pairs perfectly with Mashed Potatoes with Spinach and Cheese (page 137; pictured opposite) to create a good-for-the-soul meal.

1 6-ounce piece day-old French bread (generous ⅓ of 16-ounce loaf), crust left on, bread cut into 8 pieces
1 cup whole milk
1¾ pounds ground beef (7% to15% fat)
2 large eggs
1 medium onion, finely chopped
½ cup plus 1 tablespoon chopped fresh Italian parsley
2 teaspoons salt
1 teaspoon ground black pepper
1 teaspoon dried summer savory

All purpose flour
2 tablespoons (¼ stick) butter
1½ teaspoons olive oil
2 cups dry red wine
¼ cup tomato paste
3 cups canned beef broth

Preheat oven to 350°F. Combine bread pieces and whole milk in medium bowl, pressing on bread to submerge; let stand until milk is absorbed, about 10 minutes. Squeeze out most of milk from bread; discard milk. Place bread in large bowl. Add ground beef, eggs, finely chopped onion, ½ cup chopped Italian parsley, salt, pepper and dried summer savory and mix well. Transfer meat mixture to processor. Process until mixture is well blended and looks pasty. Form mixture into 1¾-inch-diameter meatballs (about 30). Divide meatballs between two 13x9x2-inch glass baking dishes. Bake meatballs 30 minutes. Set meatballs aside.

Dust meatballs with flour; shake off excess. Melt butter with oil in heavy large skillet over medium-high heat. Working in batches, add meatballs to skillet and sauté until brown on all sides, about 3 minutes. Return all meatballs to skillet. Whisk wine and tomato paste in small bowl to blend. Add wine mixture to meatballs and bring to boil. Continue boiling until mixture thickens slightly, stirring frequently, about 5 minutes. Add broth; reduce heat to medium and simmer until flavors blend and gravy thickens, stirring frequently, about 15 minutes. Season to taste with salt and pepper. Transfer meatballs and gravy to bowl. Sprinkle with remaining 1 tablespoon chopped Italian parsley and serve.

6 SERVINGS

Meats

Roots

The new interest in comfort food has led cooks to rediscover the pleasures of humble root vegetables.

- Beets: In addition to familiar red types, farmers' markets offer golden, pink, white, or even candy-striped heirloom varieties. To intensify their flavors, bake them instead of boiling.
- Carrots: Orange, sweet and packed with vitamin A, these are great raw or steamed, sautéed, stir-fried or braised.
- Celery Roots: Also called celeriac, these knobby relatives of celery are shredded raw for salads or cooked and mashed with potatoes.
- Parsnips: Ivory-hued, subtly sweet carrot cousins, these can be roasted with assorted vegetables or boiled and mashed like potatoes. They're also great french-fried.
- Radishes: Small and round or long, and deep red, lavender, black or white, these crisp, pungent roots are best eaten raw.
- Rutabagas: Also called swedes, these large bulbous turnip relatives have pale yellow flesh and a slightly pungent taste that's wonderful braised, roasted or pureed.
- Turnips: Mild and sweet when small and young, white-fleshed turnips are excellent simmered, braised, roasted or pureed.

Beef Stew with Winter Root Vegetables

8	ounces bacon, cut into 1-inch pieces
5	pounds beef chuck, trimmed, cut into 1½-inch pieces
½	cup all purpose flour
6	tablespoons (about) olive oil
2	pounds onions, thinly sliced
6	garlic cloves, chopped
¼	cup red wine vinegar
3	tablespoons (packed) brown sugar
2	14½-ounce cans beef broth
3	cups dark beer
1½	pounds carrots, peeled, cut into 2-inch lengths
1½	pounds parsnips, peeled, cut into 2-inch lengths
¾	cup chopped fresh parsley
2	small bay leaves
1	tablespoon chopped fresh thyme

Cook bacon in large pot over medium-high heat until brown and crisp, about 6 minutes. Using slotted spoon, transfer bacon to paper towels. Pour off all but ¼ cup drippings from pot. Place beef in large bowl. Sprinkle with flour, salt and pepper and toss to coat. Heat drippings in pot over high heat. Working in batches, add beef and brown well, adding oil by tablespoonfuls as needed, about 5 minutes per batch. Transfer to large bowl.

Heat 4 tablespoons oil in same pot over high heat. Add onions and garlic; sauté 5 minutes. Add vinegar and sugar; stir 2 minutes. Add broth; bring to boil, scraping up any browned bits. Return beef to pot. Add bacon and all remaining ingredients. Reduce heat to medium, cover and simmer until meat is tender, stirring occasionally, about 1½ hours. Season to taste with salt and pepper. (*Can be prepared 1 day ahead. Chill uncovered until cold, then cover and keep refrigerated. Rewarm over low heat before serving.*)

10 SERVINGS

42   The Flavors of Bon Appétit 2002

Steak Salad Sandwiches with Capers

    2   cups ½-inch cubes cooked steak (about 1 pound)
    2   tablespoons drained capers
    2   tablespoons chopped cornichons or gherkin pickles
    2   tablespoons minced red onion
    1   tablespoon Dijon mustard
    5   tablespoons mayonnaise

    8   ½-inch-thick slices olive or rosemary country-style bread
        (each about 3x5 inches)
    8   large tomato slices
    2   small bunches arugula, trimmed

Combine cooked steak, capers, cornichons, red onion, Dijon mustard and
2 tablespoons mayonnaise in medium bowl; toss to blend. Season salad with
salt and pepper. *(Can be prepared 6 hours ahead. Cover and refrigerate.)*

Arrange bread on work surface. Spread slices with remaining 3 tablespoons
mayonnaise. Divide steak salad among 4 bread slices. Top salad on each with
2 tomato slices and ¼ of arugula. Press second bread slice, mayonnaise side
down, onto each sandwich. Cut sandwiches diagonally in half and serve.

4 SERVINGS

Roast Beef with Rosemary Mayonnaise

    4   teaspoons finely chopped fresh rosemary
    4   teaspoons distilled white vinegar
    2   cups mayonnaise
    1   garlic clove, pressed

        Romaine lettuce leaves
    2   pounds thinly sliced roast beef
    1   red onion, thinly sliced (optional)

Place chopped rosemary and vinegar in medium bowl. Let stand 15 minutes.
Whisk in mayonnaise and garlic. Season rosemary mayonnaise to taste with
salt and pepper. *(Can be prepared 2 days ahead. Cover and refrigerate.)*

Line large platter with romaine leaves. Arrange roast beef slices atop lettuce. Sprinkle with onion slices, if desired. Serve rosemary mayonnaise
alongside platter of roast beef.

8 SERVINGS

Backpack Lunch for Four

**Steak Salad Sandwiches
with Capers**
(at left)

Carrot Sticks

Raspberry Lemonade
(page 35)

**Peanut Butter and Chocolate
"Kiss" Cookies**
(page 217)

Beef and Andouille Burgers
with Asiago Cheese

    4 oil-packed sun-dried tomatoes, drained
    ½ cup mayonnaise
    1 tablespoon whole-grain Dijon mustard

    8 ounces andouille sausages,* cut into 1-inch pieces
   2½ pounds ground beef (15% fat)
    2 large shallots, minced
    2 teaspoons salt
    2 teaspoons ground black pepper
    1 teaspoon fennel seeds, crushed

    6 large sesame-seed hamburger buns
    6 ⅓-inch-thick slices red onion
       Olive oil
    1 cup coarsely grated Asiago cheese**

    1 7- to 7½-ounce jar roasted red peppers, drained

Finely chop sun-dried tomatoes in processor. Blend in mayonnaise and mustard. Transfer to small bowl. *(Can be made 1 day ahead. Cover; chill.)*

Finely chop andouille sausages in processor. Transfer to large bowl. Add beef, shallots, salt, pepper and crushed fennel seeds. Stir with fork just until blended. Form mixture into six 1-inch-thick patties.

Prepare barbecue (medium-high heat). Grill hamburger buns until golden, about 2 minutes. Transfer to platter. Brush onion slices with oil. Sprinkle with salt and pepper. Grill until golden, about 7 minutes per side. Grill hamburgers to desired doneness, about 5 minutes per side for medium-rare. Sprinkle cheese over top of burgers.

Spread cut sides of hamburger buns with sun-dried-tomato mayonnaise. Top bottom halves of buns with hamburgers, then red peppers. Top with onion slices. Cover with top halves of buns.

Smoked pork-and-beef sausages, sold at specialty foods stores and supermarkets. Kielbasa can be substituted.
**Asiago cheese is available at specialty foods stores and some supermarkets.*

6 SERVINGS

Grilled Porterhouse Steak
with Paprika-Parmesan Butter

1   2¾- to 3-inch-thick porterhouse steak (about 2¾ pounds)
¼   cup olive oil
7   large garlic cloves, minced
1   tablespoon chopped fresh thyme
1   tablespoon salt
2   teaspoons ground black pepper
1   teaspoon chopped fresh rosemary

Paprika-Parmesan Butter (see recipe below)

Place steak in glass baking dish. Whisk oil and next 5 ingredients in small bowl to blend. Pour half of marinade over steak. Turn steak over; pour remaining marinade over steak. Cover and refrigerate at least 2 hours and up to 1 day, turning occasionally.

Prepare barbecue (medium heat). Remove steak from marinade; shake off excess. Place steak on barbecue; cover barbecue. Grill steak to desired doneness (until instant-read thermometer inserted into center of steak registers 115°F to 120°F for rare, about 15 minutes per side, or 125°F to 130°F for medium-rare, about 18 minutes per side), occasionally moving steak to cooler part of rack if burning. Transfer steak to platter; cover to keep warm. Let stand 5 minutes. Using sharp knife, cut meat away from bone. Cut each meat section into ⅓-inch-thick slices. Spread Paprika-Parmesan Butter over top of slices and serve.

4 SERVINGS

Paprika-Parmesan Butter

3   tablespoons butter, room temperature
2   teaspoons grated Parmesan cheese
1   drained anchovy fillet, minced
1   teaspoon paprika
½   teaspoon Dijon mustard
½   teaspoon Worcestershire sauce
¼   teaspoon ground black pepper
¼   teaspoon hot pepper sauce

Mix all ingredients in small bowl until blended. (*Can be prepared 2 days ahead. Chill. Bring to room temperature before using.*)

MAKES ABOUT ¼ CUP

Eclectic Asian Menu
for Six

Purchased Spring Rolls

Stir-fried Lemongrass Beef
with Asian Greens
(at right; pictured opposite)

Thai Cucumber Salad
with Roasted Peanuts
(page 138)

Steamed Rice

Japanese Beer

Green Tea Ice Cream

Stir-fried Lemongrass Beef
with Asian Greens

1½	pounds beef top sirloin, fat trimmed, cut lengthwise in half
3	tablespoons minced lemongrass
4	tablespoons fish sauce (nam pla)*
1½	tablespoons soy sauce
1½	teaspoons sugar
3	garlic cloves, minced
4	tablespoons peanut oil
3	tablespoons fresh lime juice
1	large shallot, minced
1	tablespoon minced seeded serrano chili
1	bunch mustard greens, torn into 1-inch pieces
1	head of bok choy, torn into 1-inch pieces
2	cups thinly sliced red onions
1	cup (packed) opal basil** or regular basil leaves

Freeze beef 30 minutes. Using large knife, thinly slice beef crosswise. Mix meat, lemongrass, 3 tablespoons fish sauce, soy sauce, ³/₄ teaspoon sugar and garlic in large bowl. Sprinkle generously with black pepper. Let stand at room temperature 30 minutes or chill up to 3 hours.

Whisk 3 tablespoons oil, lime juice, shallot, chili, remaining 1 tablespoon fish sauce and ³/₄ teaspoon sugar in bowl to blend. Season dressing with salt and pepper. Let stand at room temperature 30 minutes.

Place mustard greens, bok choy, onions and basil in large bowl. Add ³/₄ of dressing; toss to coat. Season salad with salt and pepper.

Heat remaining 1 tablespoon oil in heavy large skillet over high heat. Working in 2 batches, stir-fry meat until cooked to desired doneness, about 35 seconds for rare. Add meat to salad. Add remaining dressing and toss to combine. Serve immediately.

Available at Asian markets and in the Asian foods section of many supermarkets.
**Opal basil has purple leaves and a milder flavor than sweet basil. It is available at Asian markets and some supermarkets.*

6 SERVINGS

Grilled Steak with Potatoes, Radicchio and Caper-Anchovy Sauce

This beautiful dish is a new take on grilled steak. Since it includes potatoes, radicchio and sirloin, all you really need to complete the meal are bread, wine and, of course, an excellent dessert.

12 1½- to 2-inch-diameter red-skinned potatoes

 2 tablespoons plus ½ cup extra-virgin olive oil
10 fresh sage leaves, 6 left whole, 4 chopped
¼ cup drained capers
 2 anchovy fillets, chopped

 1 1-pound sirloin steak (about 2 inches thick)
    Additional olive oil

 1 small head of radicchio, thinly sliced

Cook potatoes in large pot of boiling salted water until just tender, about 10 minutes. Drain. Cut in half.

Preheat oven to 200°F. Heat 2 tablespoons oil in heavy large nonstick skillet over medium heat. Add potatoes and 6 whole sage leaves; sauté until potatoes are golden, about 12 minutes. Using slotted spoon, transfer potatoes to baking sheet. Season with salt and pepper. Keep warm in oven. Add ½ cup oil to same skillet; reduce heat to low. Add capers and anchovies and stir until warm.

Meanwhile, prepare barbecue (medium-high heat) or preheat broiler. Brush steak lightly with olive oil. Sprinkle with salt and pepper. Grill or broil steak to desired doneness, about 6 minutes per side for medium-rare.

Mound radicchio in center of each of 4 plates. Slice steak and arrange atop radicchio. Spoon potatoes alongside; sprinkle with 4 chopped sage leaves. Spoon caper-anchovy sauce over steaks.

4 SERVINGS

Veal Scallops with Creamy Mushroom Sauce

½ cup all purpose flour
1¼ pounds large veal scallops (each about ¼ inch thick)
 5 tablespoons butter

 8 ounces crimini mushrooms, sliced
 2 large shallots, finely chopped (about ½ cup)
¾ cup dry white wine
 1 cup whipping cream
 2 tablespoons chopped fresh parsley

Place flour in shallow dish. Sprinkle veal scallops with salt and pepper. Melt 2 tablespoons butter in heavy large skillet over high heat. Coat veal in flour, shaking off excess. Working in batches, add veal to skillet and sauté until beginning to brown, about 1 minute per side. Transfer to plate. Tent with foil to keep warm.

Melt remaining 3 tablespoons butter in same skillet over medium-high heat. Add mushrooms and shallots and sauté until mushrooms are brown and tender, about 7 minutes. Add wine; simmer until liquid is reduced to ¼ cup. Add cream; simmer until reduced to sauce consistency, about 3 minutes. Season sauce with salt and pepper. Return veal to skillet; simmer until just heated through, about 1 minute. Transfer veal to plates, spooning sauce over. Sprinkle with parsley; serve.

4 SERVINGS

Double-cut Veal Chops with Aromatic Pan Sauce

2	double-rib veal chops (each about 2½ inches thick)
5	tablespoons butter
1	cup chopped onion
½	cup chopped carrot
1	small bay leaf, halved
1½	teaspoons minced fresh thyme
1	garlic clove, minced
½	cup chicken stock or canned low-salt chicken broth

Sprinkle veal with salt and pepper. Melt 3 tablespoons butter in large pot over high heat. Add veal; brown on all sides, turning occasionally, about 10 minutes. Transfer veal to plate. Add onion, carrot, bay leaf, thyme and garlic to pot. Reduce heat to medium-high; sauté until vegetables are slightly softened, 5 minutes. Place chops atop vegetables; add any juices from plate, then stock. Reduce heat to medium. Cover and simmer 10 minutes. Turn chops over. Cover and cook to desired doneness, about 25 minutes longer for medium-rare (145°F to 150°F). Place veal on plate; tent with foil.

Spoon fat off top of veal-braising liquid. Press liquid and solids through strainer set over bowl to make puree; return puree to pot. Bring to boil. Whisk in remaining 2 tablespoons butter. Simmer until sauce coats spoon lightly, about 2 minutes; season with salt and pepper. Cut veal chops horizontally in half. Set on plates. Spoon sauce over and serve.

4 SERVINGS

Cold-Weather Menu for Four

Salad of Winter Greens, Walnuts, Roasted Beets and Goat Cheese
(page 141)

Double-cut Veal Chops with Aromatic Pan Sauce
(at left)

Mashed Potatoes

Steamed Broccoli Rabe

Beaujolais

Fresh Fruit and Madeleines

Grilled Spiced Lamb Chops with
Saffron Vegetables and Red Bell Pepper Sauce

This lamb entrée can provide the foundation for a Mediterranean fusion dinner. Serve it with couscous, an orange salad and sweetened tea.

LAMB

1½ cups plain whole-milk yogurt
6 tablespoons olive oil
6 tablespoons fresh lemon juice
1 tablespoon ground cardamom
1 tablespoon ground cumin
1½ teaspoons cayenne pepper
3 1½-pound racks of lamb, fat trimmed, cut into individual chops

VEGETABLES

2 tablespoons (¼ stick) butter
2 tablespoons olive oil
4 large shallots, peeled, thinly sliced
2 large leeks (white and pale green parts only), thinly sliced
¾ teaspoon saffron threads
½ teaspoon turmeric
1½ cups water
2 large turnips, peeled, cut into 1-inch pieces
2 large carrots, peeled, cut into 1-inch pieces
2 large rutabagas, peeled, cut into 1-inch pieces

Red Bell Pepper Sauce (see recipe opposite)

FOR LAMB: Whisk first 6 ingredients in medium bowl. Place chops on large rimmed baking sheet. Pour marinade over, turning to coat. Cover and refrigerate at least 1 hour and up to 3 hours.

FOR VEGETABLES: Melt butter with oil in heavy large skillet over medium heat. Add shallots, leeks, saffron and turmeric; sauté 5 minutes. Add 1½ cups water, turnips, carrots and rutabagas. Cover and simmer until vegetables are tender, stirring occasionally, about 25 minutes. Season generously with salt and pepper.

Meanwhile, prepare barbecue (medium heat). Brush grill with oil. Remove lamb from marinade, scraping off some of excess marinade. Sprinkle lamb with salt and pepper. Grill to desired doneness, about 3 minutes per side for medium-rare.

Divide grilled lamb chops among 6 plates. Serve with saffron vegetables and Red Bell Pepper Sauce.

6 SERVINGS

Red Bell Pepper Sauce

1 7-ounce jar roasted red peppers
½ cup olive oil

Puree peppers and their liquid with oil in processor. Transfer puree to heavy small saucepan. Season with salt and pepper. *(Can be prepared 2 days ahead. Cover; chill.)* Stir over medium heat until warm, about 3 minutes.

MAKES ABOUT 1 CUP

Home-Style
Dinner for Four

**Roasted Lamb Shanks with
Braised Lentils**
(at right)

Green Beans

**Whole Wheat Bread with
Raisins and Walnuts**
(page 152)

Cabernet Sauvignon

Brownies with Whipped Cream

Roasted Lamb Shanks with Braised Lentils

2½ cups chopped red onions
1 cup diced celery
1 cup diced peeled carrots
3 tablespoons chopped fresh thyme
3 tablespoons chopped fresh mint
4 large lamb shanks (about 6 pounds total)
5 tablespoons extra-virgin olive oil
8 cups chicken stock or canned low-salt chicken broth

½ cup dry red wine
4 juniper berries* (optional)
1 bay leaf
1 tablespoon all purpose flour
1 tablespoon butter, room temperature

Braised Lentils (see recipe opposite)

Preheat oven to 500°F. Spread onions, celery and carrots over bottom of large roasting pan. Rub thyme and mint over lamb shanks; sprinkle generously with salt and pepper. Place lamb shanks atop vegetables. Drizzle 3 tablespoons oil over. Roast uncovered 30 minutes. Pour 1 cup chicken stock over lamb and vegetables in pan. Reduce oven temperature to 425°F. Continue to roast uncovered until lamb is very tender and almost falls off bones, adding 1 cup stock to pan every 30 minutes and turning and basting lamb occasionally, about 3 hours longer. Using tongs, transfer lamb shanks to bowl; cover to keep warm.

Transfer vegetables and pan juices to large saucepan; skim fat from surface. Add remaining 1 cup stock, wine, juniper berries if desired, and bay leaf to saucepan. Simmer 10 minutes to blend flavors. Strain, pressing on solids to extract as much vegetable pulp and liquid as possible. Return strained liquid to same saucepan; bring to boil. Mix flour and butter to blend in small bowl. Add to saucepan; whisk until sauce thickens slightly and is reduced to 2 cups, about 2 minutes. Season sauce with salt and pepper.

Spoon Braised Lentils onto 4 plates. Drizzle remaining 2 tablespoons oil over lentils. Top each serving with 1 lamb shank. Spoon sauce over lamb.

Available in the spice section of most supermarkets.

4 SERVINGS

Braised Lentils

        3 tablespoons extra-virgin olive oil
        1 cup finely chopped red onion
      ⅔ cup finely chopped carrot
      ½ cup finely chopped celery
    1¼ cups dried green lentils
        4 cups chicken stock or canned low-salt chicken broth

Heat oil in heavy medium saucepan over medium-high heat. Add onion, carrot and celery and sauté until slightly softened, about 5 minutes. Add lentils and stir 1 minute. Add stock and bring to boil. Reduce heat to medium-low, cover and simmer until lentils are just tender, stirring occasionally, about 35 minutes. Season with salt and pepper.

4 SERVINGS

Lamb Piccata with Capers

        4 8- to 10-ounce lamb blade shoulder chops

      ½ cup all purpose flour
        5 tablespoons (about) chilled butter

      ¾ cup canned low-salt chicken broth
        3 tablespoons fresh lemon juice
        2 tablespoons drained capers

Using small sharp knife, cut around lamb bones; discard bones, leaving 3 irregular pieces of meat from each chop. Cut off fat and sinew from each piece. Place lamb between sheets of waxed paper or plastic wrap. Using meat mallet, pound lamb to ⅓-inch thickness.

Sprinkle lamb generously with salt and pepper. Coat lamb with flour; shake off excess. Melt 1 tablespoon butter in large skillet over medium-high heat. Working in batches, add lamb to skillet and cook until brown and beginning to shrink, about 2 minutes per side, adding more butter to skillet as needed. Transfer lamb to platter; cover to keep warm.

Add broth to skillet; boil until reduced to generous ⅓ cup, scraping up any browned bits, about 2 minutes. Add lemon juice. Reduce heat to medium-low; add 2 tablespoons butter, ½ tablespoon at a time, whisking until melted before adding next piece. Stir in capers. Season to taste with salt and pepper. Pour sauce over lamb and serve.

4 SERVINGS

Springtime Supper for Six

Rosemary Lamb with Pan Juices

8   large garlic cloves
2   teaspoons salt
1   6-pound leg of lamb, boned, trimmed, butterflied, bone reserved
1   tablespoon chopped fresh rosemary plus 20 large sprigs
4   tablespoons extra-virgin olive oil

3   cups water
2   lemons, thinly sliced

2   tablespoons chopped fresh parsley

Finely grind garlic and salt in processor. Place lamb, cut side up, on work surface. Sprinkle with pepper. Spread garlic-salt mixture evenly over lamb, then sprinkle with chopped rosemary. Roll lamb into its original shape. Using kitchen string, tie lamb roll crosswise every 2 inches, then tie lengthwise. Slide rosemary sprigs under string to cover both sides of lamb. Place lamb in 13x9-inch baking dish. Drizzle oil all over lamb. Cover with plastic wrap and refrigerate 1 day.

Preheat oven to 350°F. Transfer lamb to large roasting pan. Sprinkle with salt and pepper. Place reserved lamb bone alongside; pour 1 cup water into pan. Arrange lemon slices from 1 lemon atop lamb. Roast lamb 1 hour. Turn lamb over; pour 1 cup water into pan. Continue to roast lamb until meat thermometer inserted into thickest part registers 140°F, about 1 hour longer. Transfer lamb to cutting board; let rest 15 minutes. Add remaining 1 cup water to pan, scraping up browned bits. Pour pan juices into 2-cup measuring cup; spoon off fat and discard. Transfer pan juices and any accumulated juices from roast lamb to small saucepan. Bring juices to simmer. Season pan juices to taste with pepper.

Discard string and rosemary from lamb. Slice lamb; place on platter. Spoon pan juices over. Garnish with parsley and remaining lemon slices.

6 SERVINGS

Orange- and Lime-marinated Lamb Kebabs

   1   3½-pound boneless leg of lamb, all fat and sinew trimmed, meat cut
         into 1¼- to 1½-inch cubes
   ¾   cup orange juice
   ½   cup olive oil
   ¼   cup fresh lime juice
   ¼   cup soy sauce
   1   tablespoon chopped fresh oregano
   1   tablespoon chopped canned chipotle chilies*
   3   garlic cloves, minced
   2   teaspoons grated lime peel
   2   teaspoons ground cumin
   2   teaspoons ground black pepper
   1   teaspoon salt

   1   red onion, cut into 1-inch pieces
   3   fresh poblano chilies,** seeded, cut into 1-inch pieces
   6   12-inch metal skewers

Place lamb cubes in large resealable plastic bag. Whisk orange juice and
next 10 ingredients in medium bowl to blend. Pour over lamb in plastic
bag. Seal bag and refrigerate overnight, turning occasionally. Drain lamb.

   Prepare barbecue (medium-high heat). Alternate 4 lamb cubes, 4 onion
pieces and 4 chili pieces on each skewer. Grill lamb to desired doneness,
turning frequently, about 9 minutes for medium-rare. Place skewers on
platter and serve.

*Chipotle chilies canned in a
spicy tomato sauce, sometimes
called adobo, are available at
Latin American markets and
some supermarkets.
**Fresh green chilies, also
called pasillas; available at
Latin American markets and
some supermarkets.

6 SERVINGS

Many foods benefit from marinating—that is, soaking in a seasoned
mixture that usually contains salt
and an acid such as vinegar or citrus
juice to flavor and tenderize. The
length of time food should be marinated, however, depends on two
main factors: the type of ingredient
and food safety.

   In general, tougher ingredients
can marinate longer, and more tender or delicate ingredients need less
time. Tough cuts of meat such as
stewing beef gain tenderness and
flavor from marinating at least
overnight in the refrigerator.
Tender seafood or poultry requires
no more than an hour or two, and
often less than half an hour, since
prolonged exposure to acids can
turn it mushy.

   To avoid growth of harmful bacteria when marinating, remember
never to leave animal proteins at
room temperature longer than two
hours. Marinating should always be
done in a covered glass, ceramic or
stainless steel container in the
refrigerator. And never baste
cooked or cooking foods with a
used marinade without first bring-
ing it to a full boil to kill off any
food-borne bacteria that may be
present. For more food safety infor-
mation, call the U. S. Department
of Agriculture Meat and Poultry
Hotline at 800-535-4555.

Rack of Lamb with Pesto

Serve this elegant main course with oven-roasted chunks of red-skinned potato sprinkled with chives; steamed baby carrots; and a limestone lettuce salad. Finish with a strawberry-rhubarb pie.

½ cup (packed) fresh parsley leaves and stems
2 tablespoons chopped fresh rosemary
2 tablespoons grated Parmesan cheese
1 garlic clove
3 tablespoons olive oil

1 1½-pound rack of lamb
Fresh rosemary sprigs

Position rack in center of oven and preheat to 450°F. Process parsley, chopped rosemary, Parmesan and garlic in processor to coarse paste. With machine running, gradually add oil. Season with salt and pepper.

Place lamb on small rimmed baking sheet. Sprinkle with salt and pepper. Spread all pesto over rounded side of lamb. Roast 10 minutes. Reduce oven temperature to 400°F and roast to desired doneness, about 15 minutes longer for medium-rare. Cut lamb between bones into chops. Divide chops between 2 plates; garnish with rosemary sprigs and serve.

2 SERVINGS

Spice-rubbed Butterflied Leg of Lamb

½ large onion, cut into 2-inch pieces
6 garlic cloves, peeled
2 tablespoons fresh mint leaves
2 tablespoons paprika
1 tablespoon salt
1 tablespoon fresh marjoram leaves
2 teaspoons ground black pepper
2 teaspoons ground cumin
2 teaspoons ground coriander
2 teaspoons hot pepper sauce
1 teaspoon turmeric
½ teaspoon ground ginger
¼ teaspoon ground cinnamon
½ cup olive oil
⅓ cup fresh lemon juice

1 4½- to 5-pound boneless leg of lamb, butterflied, fat and sinew trimmed

To make this dish easy, ask your butcher to bone, butterfly and trim the lamb for you. And remember to start a day ahead of time.

Combine first 13 ingredients in processor. Using on/off turns, process until coarse paste forms. Add oil and lemon juice and process until well blended.

Place lamb in large resealable plastic bag. Pour spice mixture over lamb; seal bag. Turn bag several times and rub spice mixture into lamb. Chill overnight, turning bag occasionally.

Prepare barbecue (medium heat). Remove lamb from marinade; shake off excess. Grill lamb to desired doneness or until instant-read thermometer inserted into thickest part of lamb registers 125°F to 130°F for medium-rare, about 15 minutes per side. Transfer lamb to cutting board. Cover with foil and let stand 5 to 10 minutes. Cut lamb into ⅓-inch-thick slices. Arrange on platter and serve.

6 TO 8 SERVINGS

Cumin-dusted Pork Cutlets with Citrus Pan Sauce

    2 tablespoons all purpose flour
    2 teaspoons ground cumin
    ½ teaspoon salt
    ½ teaspoon ground black pepper
    4 pork cutlets (about 12 ounces total)
    3 tablespoons olive oil
    2 garlic cloves, minced
    ¼ cup fresh orange juice
    3 tablespoons fresh lemon juice
       Orange wedges

Mix first 4 ingredients on plate. Coat pork in seasoned flour, shaking off excess. Heat 1 tablespoon oil in large nonstick skillet over medium-high heat. Add pork; sauté until cooked through, about 3 minutes per side. Transfer to 2 plates. Add 2 tablespoons oil to skillet. Add garlic; sauté until golden, about 10 seconds. Add orange juice and lemon juice. Boil until slightly thickened, whisking occasionally, about 30 seconds. Season with salt and pepper. Pour sauce over pork. Garnish with orange wedges; serve.

2 SERVINGS

Slow-baked Spareribs with Mango-Chutney Marinade

    2 racks pork spareribs (about 6½ pounds)
    1 cup dry Sherry
    ½ cup soy sauce
    ¼ cup oriental sesame oil
    ¼ cup mango chutney
    2 tablespoons honey
    2 green onions, finely chopped
    1 tablespoon finely chopped peeled fresh ginger
    4 large garlic cloves, minced
    1 teaspoon cayenne pepper

Arrange rib racks in large roasting pan. Whisk all remaining ingredients in medium bowl to blend. Pour marinade over ribs, turning to coat. Cover and refrigerate overnight, turning ribs once.

Position 1 oven rack in top third of oven and 1 rack in bottom third of oven; preheat to 300°F. Drain ribs; reserve marinade. Transfer marinade to saucepan; bring to boil. Remove from heat. Place each rack of ribs on large rimmed baking sheet. Place 1 baking sheet on each rack in oven. Bake ribs until tender, basting with ¼ cup marinade every 20 minutes and covering edges of ribs with strips of foil to protect from burning if necessary, about 3 hours total. Cut between bones to separate ribs. Transfer to platter; serve.

4 SERVINGS

Roast Pork Loin with Pumpkin-Seed Sauce

A tamarind is a legume with large brown seedpods. The distinctive sweet-sour pulp is used in Indian, Thai, Caribbean and Latin American cooking. Tamarind pulp is sold in block form and is available at Indian markets. Frozen pulp is available at Latin American and Asian markets.

3 ounces dried tamarind pulp
1 cup hot water
2 12-ounce pork tenderloins

½ cup shelled pumpkin seeds (pepitas)*
3 tablespoons vegetable oil
1 cup chopped husked tomatillos* (about 4 ounces)
½ cup chopped onion
1 jalapeño chili, seeded, chopped
1 small garlic clove, minced
2½ cups chicken stock or canned low-salt chicken broth
2 cups chopped romaine lettuce
¼ cup toasted walnuts (about 2 ounces), ground
¼ cup toasted almonds (about 2 ounces), ground

Place tamarind pulp and 1 cup hot water in small bowl. Let stand until tamarind is soft, about 2 hours. Strain into medium bowl, pressing to extract as much pulp as possible. Discard solids in strainer. Place pork in bowl with liquid. Cover and chill at least 2 hours and up to 1 day.

Stir seeds in medium skillet over medium-high heat until beginning to pop, 5 minutes. Cool. Transfer to processor and blend until ground. Transfer to bowl. Heat 2 tablespoons oil in heavy large skillet over high heat. Add tomatillos, onion, jalapeño and garlic. Sauté until onion is slightly softened, about 3 minutes. Add 1 cup stock. Reduce heat to medium; cover and simmer until tomatillos are soft, about 5 minutes. Cool slightly. Puree half of tomatillo mixture with lettuce in blender until smooth. Pour into large bowl. Add remaining tomatillo mixture to blender and puree until smooth. Add ground seeds, walnuts and almonds to blender and process just until blended. Mix into tomatillo-lettuce puree in bowl.

Heat 1 tablespoon oil in large skillet over medium-high heat. Add nut sauce and 1½ cups stock. Bring to boil. Reduce heat to medium-low and simmer until thick, 10 minutes. Season with salt and pepper.

Prepare barbecue (medium-high heat). Preheat oven to 400°F. Remove pork from marinade. Sprinkle with salt and pepper. Grill pork until dark brown, turning occasionally, about 10 minutes. Transfer pork to small rimmed baking sheet. Roast in oven until cooked through, about 20 minutes for medium. Let pork rest 5 minutes. Cut into 1-inch cubes.

Rewarm sauce; spoon onto 4 plates. Top with pork.

*Available at Latin American markets and some supermarkets.

4 SERVINGS

Beer-brined Grilled Pork Chops

> 2 cups water
> 2 cups dark lager beer
> ¼ cup coarse salt
> 3 tablespoons (packed) dark brown sugar
> 3 tablespoons mild-flavored (light) molasses
> 1 cup ice cubes
> 6 1- to 1¼-inch-thick center-cut bone-in pork chops
>
> 7 large garlic cloves, minced
> 3 teaspoons coarsely ground black pepper
> 2 teaspoons salt
> 2 teaspoons dried sage leaves

Combine 2 cups water, beer, ¼ cup coarse salt, sugar and molasses in large bowl. Stir until salt and sugar dissolve. Stir in ice. Place pork chops in large resealable plastic bag. Pour beer brine over pork chops; seal bag. Refrigerate 4 hours, turning bag occasionally.

Prepare barbecue (medium-high heat). Remove pork chops from beer brine; pat dry. Mix garlic and next 3 ingredients in small bowl. Rub garlic mixture over both sides of pork chops. Grill pork chops until instant-read thermometer inserted into center of chops registers 145°F to 150°F, about 10 minutes per side, occasionally moving chops to cooler part of rack if burning. Transfer chops to platter; cover with foil and let stand 5 minutes. Serve.

6 SERVINGS

Saturday Evening Supper for Six

Blue Cheese and Caramelized Shallot Dip
(page 12)

Beer-brined Grilled Pork Chops
(at left)

Baked Potatoes

Grilled Zucchini and Baby Eggplant

Beer

Raspberry Sorbet

Chicken and Root Vegetable Stew

Serve a Sauvignon Blanc to complement the flavors of this delicious make-ahead stew.

2 tablespoons olive oil
12 chicken thighs, well trimmed
2 cups chopped onions
6 garlic cloves, chopped
1 cup dry white wine
¼ cup plus 2 tablespoons chopped fresh marjoram
2 large boiling potatoes, peeled, each cut into 12 pieces
3 large carrots, peeled, cut into ½-inch-thick rounds
2 large parsnips, peeled, cut into ½-inch-thick rounds
2 medium rutabagas, peeled, cut into 1½-inch pieces
2 medium turnips, peeled, cut into 1½-inch pieces
5 cups canned low-salt chicken broth

¾ cup whipping cream
2 tablespoons cornstarch

Heat oil in heavy large pot over medium-high heat. Working in batches, add chicken and cook until brown on all sides, about 8 minutes per batch; transfer browned chicken to large bowl. Pour off all but 2 tablespoons drippings from pot. Add onions to pot and sauté over medium heat until golden, about 8 minutes. Add garlic and sauté 1 minute. Add wine and ¼ cup marjoram and simmer until wine evaporates, about 4 minutes. Return chicken to pot. Arrange vegetables over chicken. Pour chicken broth over. Cover and bring to boil. Reduce heat and simmer until chicken is cooked through and vegetables are tender, about 30 minutes.

Using slotted spoon, carefully transfer chicken and vegetables to large clean bowl. Boil liquid in pot until reduced to 3 cups, about 10 minutes. Mix cream and cornstarch in medium bowl. Stir into liquid in pot. Simmer until thickened to sauce consistency, about 5 minutes. Return chicken and vegetables to pot. *(Can be made 2 days ahead. Cool slightly, then refrigerate uncovered until cold. Cover and keep refrigerated.)* Bring stew to simmer, stirring gently. Add remaining 2 tablespoons marjoram and serve.

6 SERVINGS

Italian Sausage and Wild Mushroom Risotto

2 tablespoons olive oil
1 pound Italian sweet sausage, casings removed, crumbled into ½-inch pieces
8 ounces portobello mushrooms, stemmed, dark gills scraped out, caps diced
10 ounces fresh shiitake mushrooms, stemmed, diced
1 teaspoon chopped fresh thyme
1 teaspoon chopped fresh oregano
1½ cups Madeira

6 cups chicken stock or canned low-salt chicken broth
½ cup (1 stick) butter
1 large onion, chopped
4 garlic cloves, minced
2 cups arborio rice or other medium-grain rice (about 13 ounces)
1 cup freshly grated Asiago cheese*

Removing the gills from the portobello mushrooms helps preserve the colors in this dish, since the gills can discolor other ingredients.

Heat oil in large nonstick skillet over medium-high heat. Add sausage and sauté until beginning to brown, about 3 minutes. Add all mushrooms, thyme and oregano; sauté until mushrooms are tender, about 10 minutes. Add ½ cup Madeira; boil until almost absorbed, about 1 minute. Set aside.

Bring stock to simmer in large saucepan; remove from heat and cover to keep hot. Melt butter in heavy large pot over medium-high heat. Add onion and garlic; sauté until onion is translucent, about 5 minutes. Add rice; stir 2 minutes. Add remaining 1 cup Madeira; simmer until absorbed, about 2 minutes. Add 1 cup hot stock; simmer until almost absorbed, stirring often, about 3 minutes. Continue to cook until rice is just tender and mixture is creamy, adding more stock by cupfuls, stirring often and allowing most stock to be absorbed before adding more, about 25 minutes. Stir in sausage mixture. Season to taste with salt and pepper. Transfer to serving bowl. Pass cheese separately.

Available at specialty foods stores and some supermarkets.

4 SERVINGS

Baked Pork Chops
with Parmesan-Sage Crust

1½ cups fresh breadcrumbs made from crustless French bread
1 cup freshly grated Parmesan cheese (about 3 ounces)
1 tablespoon dried rubbed sage
1 teaspoon grated lemon peel
2 large eggs
¼ cup all purpose flour
4 bone-in center-cut pork loin chops (each about 1 inch thick)

2 tablespoons (¼ stick) butter
2 tablespoons olive oil
   Lemon wedges (optional)
   Orange wedges (optional)

Preheat oven to 425°F. Mix breadcrumbs, cheese, sage and lemon peel in pie dish. Whisk eggs in medium bowl to blend. Place flour on plate; season generously with salt and pepper. Coat pork chops on both sides with flour; shake off excess flour. Dip chops into eggs, then coat on both sides with breadcrumb mixture.

Melt butter with oil in heavy large ovenproof skillet over medium-high heat. Add pork chops to skillet and cook until golden brown, about 2 minutes per side. Transfer skillet with pork to oven. Bake until pork chops are crisp on outside and meat thermometer inserted into pork registers 150°F, about 20 minutes. Transfer pork chops to plates. Garnish with lemon wedges and orange wedges, if desired, and serve.

4 SERVINGS

Poultry

Chicken Sauté
with Olives and Plum Tomatoes

2½ tablespoons olive oil
2 6-ounce skinless boneless chicken breast halves
3 tablespoons chopped fresh marjoram
1 yellow bell pepper, thinly sliced
5 garlic cloves, minced
1½ cups seeded diced plum tomatoes
¼ cup coarsely chopped pitted Kalamata or other brine-cured black olives

Heat 1½ tablespoons oil in heavy medium skillet over medium heat. Sprinkle chicken on both sides with salt, pepper and 1 tablespoon marjoram. Add to skillet; sauté until golden, about 4 minutes per side. Transfer chicken to plate. Add 1 tablespoon oil to skillet. Add bell pepper; sauté 2 minutes. Add garlic; sauté 1 minute. Add tomatoes; sauté until juices are released, about 3 minutes. Stir in olives and remaining 2 tablespoons marjoram. Return chicken to skillet. Reduce heat to medium-low, cover and simmer until chicken is cooked through, about 2 minutes. Season with salt and pepper.

2 SERVINGS

Spoon some of the sauce over noodles that have been tossed with Parmesan cheese, and serve with a salad of balsamic-dressed *mesclun* and crusty bread. Finish the meal with almond cookies and grapes.

Stir-fried Chicken Wraps
with Radishes, Chipotles and Lime

9	large skinless boneless chicken thighs, fat trimmed, chicken cut into ½-inch pieces
4	tablespoons fresh lime juice
1½	teaspoons crushed chipotle chilies*
6	teaspoons olive oil
9	green onions (white and pale green parts only), thinly sliced
½	cup canned low-salt chicken broth
18	radishes, trimmed, halved, thinly sliced crosswise, and 20 radish leaves, thinly sliced, reserved
2	tablespoons chopped fresh cilantro
	Lime wedges
12	hot corn tortillas

Combine chicken, 1½ tablespoons lime juice and crushed chipotles in large bowl. Sprinkle with salt and pepper; toss to blend. Let stand 10 minutes. Heat 4 teaspoons oil in large nonstick skillet over high heat. Add chicken mixture and sauté 3 minutes. Stir in green onions and broth; cover and cook 3 minutes. Uncover and stir until chicken is cooked through and most liquid evaporates, about 2 minutes longer. Stir in 1½ tablespoons lime juice. Season with salt and pepper. Transfer to bowl; cover to keep warm.

Heat remaining 2 teaspoons oil in same skillet over high heat. Add radish slices and sauté 1 minute. Stir in remaining 1 tablespoon lime juice. Season with salt and pepper. Add radish slices and cilantro to bowl with chicken and toss to blend.

Divide chicken mixture among 6 tortillas. Sprinkle with reserved sliced radish leaves and roll up. Garnish with lime wedges.

Crushed chipotle chilies (dried smoked jalapeño chilies) are available at Latin American markets and in the spice section of some supermarkets.

6 SERVINGS

What's So Hot?

From New Orleans to India, Korea to Jamaica, the ground red chili known as cayenne sets cooks' imaginations and mouths afire. Rating up to 8 on a culinary heat scale that starts at 1 and peaks at 10, the pepper also contributes tart, smoky flavor.

Chili aficionados can get different tastes by substituting other forms of ground red pepper. Try the following powdered chilies.

- *Ancho:* Sweet, slightly fruity, and with a heat level no more than 5 on the heat scale.
- Chipotle: Smoky-sweet and well-rounded, this form of smoke-dried jalapeño has a heat level of 5 to 6.
- New Mexico: Fruity and earthy, with heat as high as 4 for the red variety.
- Paprika: Popular in Spanish and Hungarian cooking, this piquant, fruity chili ranges from a heat level of 3 or so (in its sweet, mild form) up to about 7.
- Indian Paprika: Indian paprika is made from dried seedless ground sweet peppers grown in India, making it similar to the mild Hungarian paprika; its heat goes up to level 3. It's often fried in oil with other spices to release its sweetness and aroma.
- *Poblano:* Fruity and herbaceous with a hint of licorice and a heat level up to 5.
- Serrano: Citrusy, with a heat level between 7 and 8.

Sunday Dinner for Four

Roast Chicken with Herb Butter, Onions and Garlic
(at right; pictured on page 38)

Green Beans

Cream Biscuits with Bacon and Roasted Onions
(page 157)

Chardonnay

Gingerbread Squares with Honey-Mascarpone Cream
(page 188)

Roast Chicken with Herb Butter, Onions and Garlic

7	tablespoons unsalted butter, room temperature
1	tablespoon chopped fresh parsley plus 3 large sprigs
1	tablespoon chopped fresh thyme plus 3 large sprigs
1	tablespoon chopped fresh rosemary plus 3 small sprigs
¼	teaspoon fennel seeds, crushed
½	teaspoon coarse salt
1	7- to 7¼-pound roasting chicken, rinsed, patted dry
3	medium onions, peeled, quartered lengthwise (do not remove root end)
14	garlic cloves, peeled
1	cup canned low-salt chicken broth
½	cup dry white wine
1½	teaspoons all purpose flour

Mix butter, chopped herbs, fennel seeds and salt in bowl; blend well. (*Can be prepared 1 day ahead. Cover and chill. Bring to room temperature before continuing.*) Position rack in bottom third of oven; preheat to 400°F. Sprinkle main cavity of chicken with salt and pepper; fill with herb sprigs. Starting at neck end, slide fingers under skin of breast and upper part of legs, loosening skin. Spread 3 tablespoons herb butter under skin on breast and upper leg meat. Place chicken on rack in roasting pan; tie legs together loosely to hold shape. Scatter onions around chicken. Brush chicken and onions with 2 tablespoons herb butter; sprinkle with salt and pepper.

Roast chicken 30 minutes. Take pan from oven. Scatter garlic around chicken. Brush chicken, onions and garlic with 1 tablespoon herb butter. Roast chicken and vegetables 30 minutes. Reserve 1 tablespoon herb butter for sauce; brush remainder on chicken and vegetables. Roast until thermometer inserted into thickest part of thigh registers 180°F, 30 minutes longer. Insert spoon into main cavity; tilt chicken so juices drain into pan. Transfer chicken to platter; surround with onions and garlic. Tent with foil.

Set roasting pan over medium-high heat. Add broth and wine; bring to simmer, scraping up browned bits. Pour pan juices into large glass measuring cup. Spoon off and discard fat. Pour juices into medium saucepan. Stir reserved 1 tablespoon herb butter and flour in small bowl to smooth paste. Bring pan juices to simmer; whisk in paste. Simmer sauce until slightly thickened, whisking occasionally, about 4 minutes. Season with salt and pepper. Serve chicken with sauce.

4 SERVINGS

Lemon-Tarragon Chicken Salad Sandwiches

1¼ pounds skinless boneless chicken breast halves (about 3)
¾ cup finely chopped celery
½ cup plus 3 tablespoons mayonnaise
¼ cup finely chopped red onion
2 tablespoons chopped fresh tarragon
2 tablespoons fresh lemon juice
1 teaspoon grated lemon peel
12 slices rye bread with seeds
2 cups thinly sliced romaine lettuce

Bring large saucepan of salted water to boil. Add chicken; reduce heat, cover and simmer until chicken is cooked through, 12 minutes. Transfer to plate; cool. Mix celery, ½ cup mayonnaise and next 4 ingredients in large bowl. Cut chicken into ½-inch cubes; stir into mayonnaise mixture. Season to taste.

Arrange 6 bread slices on work surface. Spread with 3 tablespoons mayonnaise. Divide salad among bread slices. Top each with lettuce and second bread slice. Cut sandwiches in half and serve.

6 SERVINGS

Buttermilk Fried Chicken

2 3- to 3¼-pound chickens, each cut into 8 pieces
1 quart buttermilk
3 cups all purpose flour
4½ teaspoons salt
4½ teaspoons black pepper
4½ teaspoons cayenne pepper
Vegetable oil

Combine chicken pieces and buttermilk in large bowl. Chill at least 1 hour and up to 1 day. Combine flour, salt, black pepper and cayenne pepper in medium bowl; whisk. Lift 1 chicken piece from buttermilk. Roll in flour mixture to coat. Place on waxed paper. Repeat with remaining chicken.

Place rack over rimmed baking sheet. Add vegetable oil to large pot to depth of 2 inches. Heat oil over medium heat to 325°F. Working in batches, add 4 chicken pieces to pot and fry until brown and cooked through, about 12 to 15 minutes. Drain chicken. Sprinkle with salt and pepper. Let stand until just cool. *(Can be prepared up to 4 hours ahead; cover and refrigerate.)*

6 TO 8 SERVINGS

Grilled Chicken, Red Onion and Mint Kebabs with Greek Salad

1½	pounds skinless boneless chicken breast halves, cut into 1-inch pieces
4	tablespoons extra-virgin olive oil
4	garlic cloves, crushed
1	teaspoon dried mint
1	teaspoon dried oregano
1	teaspoon salt
1	teaspoon ground black pepper
2	tablespoons fresh lemon juice
1	bunch fresh mint
1	red onion, cut into 1-inch pieces
8	12-inch metal skewers
	Greek Salad (see recipe below)

Mix chicken, 2 tablespoons oil, garlic, mint, oregano, salt and pepper in medium bowl. Let marinate 30 minutes. Whisk remaining 2 tablespoons oil and lemon juice in small bowl to blend. Prepare barbecue (medium-high heat). Pull off large mint leaves from stems. Alternate chicken, onion and mint leaves on skewers; sprinkle with salt and pepper. Grill until chicken is just cooked through, turning and basting occasionally with oil-lemon mixture, about 9 minutes. Serve Greek Salad alongside.

4 SERVINGS

Greek Salad

¾	pound tomatoes, seeded, diced (about 2 cups)
2	cups diced seeded peeled cucumber (from about 1 large)
1	cup diced red bell pepper (from about 1 large)
¼	cup pitted Kalamata olives or other brine-cured black olives, halved
¼	cup diced red onion
3	tablespoons chopped fresh Italian parsley
3	tablespoons extra-virgin olive oil
1½	tablespoons red wine vinegar
½	teaspoon dried oregano
¼	cup crumbled feta cheese (about 2 ounces)

Toss first 9 ingredients in bowl to blend. Mix in cheese. Season with salt and pepper. (*Can be made 2 hours ahead. Let stand at room temperature.*)

MAKES ABOUT 4½ CUPS

Tandoori-Style Grilled Chicken

This recipe adapts traditional Indian tandoori cooking to the barbecue. The chicken needs to marinate overnight, so start this a day ahead.

2 cups plain whole-milk yogurt
2 tablespoons fresh lemon juice
2 tablespoons minced peeled fresh ginger
4 garlic cloves, minced
1 teaspoon salt
1 teaspoon ground coriander
1 teaspoon ground turmeric
½ teaspoon saffron threads, crumbled
½ teaspoon ground cumin
½ teaspoon ground black pepper
½ teaspoon cayenne pepper
8 skinless leg-thigh chicken pieces

3 tablespoons butter, melted
1 small red onion, thinly sliced crosswise, separated into rings
¼ cup chopped fresh cilantro

Blend 1 cup yogurt and next 10 ingredients in processor until smooth. Transfer to large bowl. Mix in remaining 1 cup yogurt. Add chicken and turn to coat. Cover and refrigerate overnight.

Prepare barbecue (medium-high heat). Place marinade-coated chicken on barbecue. Grill chicken until just cooked through, occasionally basting with butter last 2 minutes, about 12 minutes per side. Transfer chicken to platter. Top with onion and cilantro and serve.

8 SERVINGS

Cornish Game Hens
with Dried Fruit and Honey

    3 tablespoons olive oil
    ½ cup blanched almonds

    2 medium onions, thinly sliced
    2 1¾-pound Cornish game hens, quartered
    2 cups water
    ½ cup finely chopped fresh parsley
    2 tablespoons minced peeled fresh ginger
    1 teaspoon ground cinnamon
    ½ teaspoon ground nutmeg
    ⅛ teaspoon ground cloves

    ½ cup honey
    1 cup mixed dried fruit (such as pitted dates, pitted prunes, and apricots),
       halved if large
    ⅓ cup raisins

Heat 2 tablespoons oil in heavy medium skillet over medium heat. Add almonds; sauté until golden, about 8 minutes. Turn almonds out onto paper towels and drain. (*Almonds can be prepared up to 2 days ahead. Store airtight at room temperature.*)

Heat remaining 1 tablespoon oil in heavy large pot over medium-high heat. Add onions and sauté until beginning to brown, about 10 minutes. Add game hens, 2 cups water, parsley, ginger, cinnamon, nutmeg and cloves and bring to boil. Reduce heat to medium-low. Cover and simmer until game hens are cooked through, turning once, about 35 minutes. Using tongs, transfer game hen pieces to bowl.

Spoon off fat from juices in pot. Add honey, dried fruit and raisins and simmer until fruit is tender, about 15 minutes. Return hen pieces to sauce. Season to taste with salt and pepper. (*Can be prepared 1 day ahead. Cool slightly. Refrigerate uncovered until cold, then cover and keep refrigerated.*) Rewarm game hens in sauce over medium-low heat. Transfer to large platter. Sprinkle with almonds and serve.

4 SERVINGS

Moroccan-inspired Menu for Four

Spinach Salad

Cornish Game Hens with Dried Fruit and Honey
(*at left*)

Couscous

Red Wine

Rustic Plum Tart
(*page 169*)

Cornish Game Hens
with Crab Apple-Sage Glaze

Serve these festive birds with roasted broccoli (as easy as steamed) and a wild rice pilaf with sliced green onions. Finish with caramel ice cream topped with chocolate sauce and chopped walnuts.

2   1¾-pound Cornish game hens, halved
8   fresh sage leaves

⅔   cup dry white wine
3   tablespoons crab apple jelly
3   tablespoons chopped shallots
2   tablespoons chopped fresh sage

Preheat oven to 450°F. Starting at neck end of hens, slide fingers between skin and breasts to loosen skin. Place 2 sage leaves under skin of each breast half. Sprinkle hens with salt and pepper. Transfer hens, skin side up, to medium roasting pan. Roast hens 15 minutes.

Meanwhile, simmer ⅓ cup wine, jelly and shallots in heavy small saucepan until glaze is slightly thickened, about 6 minutes. Stir in chopped sage.

Brush half of glaze on roasted hens. Roast hens 5 minutes longer. Brush with remaining glaze. Roast until hens are cooked through and glaze is bubbling, about 5 minutes longer. Transfer to platter.

Spoon off fat from juices in pan. Place pan directly atop 2 burners over medium heat. Add remaining ⅓ cup wine; boil until liquid is reduced by ⅓, about 5 minutes. Season sauce with salt and pepper. Spoon over hens.

4 SERVINGS

Spiced Lacquered Duck

This dish blends the spices of two cuisines: Asian (Chinese five-spice powder) and Creole (cayenne). Marinate the duck two days ahead. Serve it with simple steamed white rice and braised baby bok choy.

1   cup soy sauce
2   tablespoons dry Sherry
2   tablespoons (packed) dark brown sugar
2   tablespoons honey
2   tablespoons hoisin sauce*
2   large garlic cloves, minced
1   tablespoon oriental sesame oil
1   teaspoon Chinese five-spice powder**
½   teaspoon cayenne pepper
1   5-pound duck, thawed if frozen, rinsed

Combine first 9 ingredients in medium bowl; whisk to blend. Place duck in jumbo resealable plastic bag. Pour in soy mixture. Seal bag; turn to coat duck. Refrigerate 2 days, turning occasionally.

Preheat oven to 400°F. Drain duck well; discard marinade. Arrange duck, breast side up, on rack set on rimmed baking sheet. Pat duck dry inside and out with paper towels. Roast duck 45 minutes. Turn over. Roast until tender and glazed deep brown, about 15 minutes. Insert wooden spoon into main cavity of duck and tilt, allowing juices to drain onto baking sheet. Transfer duck to platter. Let rest 15 minutes before serving.

*Available at Asian markets and in the Asian foods section of most supermarkets.
**A blend of ground anise, cinnamon, star anise, cloves and ginger, available in the spice section of most supermarkets.*

4 SERVINGS

Duck Breasts with Coriander, Endive and Sweet-and-Sour Orange Sauce

A brilliant blend of French and Asian flavors, this delicious entrée can be made in stages, beginning with the endive and sauce prepared a day ahead and ending with the roasting of the duck just before serving.

ENDIVE

12 small heads of Belgian endive
 1 tablespoon sugar
⅛ teaspoon salt
¾ cup fresh orange juice
¾ cup chicken stock or canned low-salt chicken broth

SAUCE

½ cup red wine vinegar
¼ cup sugar
 1 tablespoon whole coriander seeds
1¼ cups fresh orange juice
 1 cup chicken stock or canned low-salt chicken broth
½ teaspoon grated orange peel

DUCK

 4 duck breasts (each about 7 ounces), excess skin trimmed
 1 tablespoon unsalted butter
 1 tablespoon olive oil
 2 tablespoons honey
 4 tablespoons whole coriander seeds, coarsely crushed

FOR ENDIVE: Arrange endive in single layer in heavy large skillet; sprinkle with sugar and salt. Add juice and stock; bring to boil. Reduce heat to medium-low. Cover; simmer 15 minutes. Turn endive over. Cover; simmer until tender, about 10 minutes longer. Using tongs, transfer endive to plate, draining juices back into skillet. Boil juices in skillet until reduced almost to glaze, whisking occasionally, about 9 minutes. Season juices with salt and pepper. Return endive to skillet.

FOR SAUCE: Stir vinegar, sugar and coriander seeds in heavy small saucepan over low heat until sugar dissolves. Increase heat and boil (do not stir) until syrup is dark at edge of pan and bubbles break thickly on surface, swirling pan occasionally, about 5 minutes. Carefully add juice and stock; boil until sauce is reduced to 1 cup, stirring often, about 12 minutes. Strain sauce into another small saucepan. Add peel. Simmer until sauce is reduced to ½ cup, about 3 minutes. (*Endive and sauce can be prepared 1 day ahead. Cover separately; chill.*)

FOR DUCK: Preheat oven to 425°F. Sprinkle duck with salt and pepper. Melt butter with oil in heavy large ovenproof skillet over high heat. Add duck, skin side down; cook until skin is very crisp, about 5 minutes. Using tongs, transfer duck, skin side down, to work surface. Brush meat side of each duck breast with 1/2 tablespoon honey. Press 1/2 tablespoon coriander seeds into honey on each breast. Discard fat from skillet. Return duck, skin side up, to skillet. Press 1/2 tablespoon coriander seeds onto skin of each breast.

Place duck in oven and roast until cooked to desired doneness, about 7 minutes for medium-rare (150°F to 160°F). Rewarm endive in covered skillet. Transfer duck to work surface. Brush most seeds off duck. Cut each breast crosswise into thin slices. Overlap slices of 1 breast on each plate. Spoon sauce over. Set 3 heads of endive on each plate.

4 SERVINGS

Southwestern Turkey Burgers

    10 ounces ground turkey
    1/2 cup plus 2 tablespoons chopped green onions
    6   tablespoons chopped fresh cilantro
    2   teaspoons minced canned chipotle chilies*
    2   teaspoons ground cumin

    2   9- to 10-inch flour tortillas
    4   tablespoons purchased guacamole
        Purchased fresh salsa

Gently mix turkey, 1/2 cup green onions, 4 tablespoons cilantro, chipotle chilies and cumin in medium bowl. Form into two 7-inch-long by 2 1/2-inch-wide patties. (Can be prepared 8 hours ahead. Cover and chill.)

Prepare barbecue (medium-high heat). Grill burgers until cooked through, about 5 minutes per side. Wrap tortillas in foil; grill until heated through. Unwrap tortillas; transfer to 2 plates. Spread 2 tablespoons guacamole down center of each tortilla. Place burgers atop guacamole. Sprinkle with remaining 2 tablespoons green onions and 2 tablespoons cilantro. Fold each tortilla to partially enclose burger. Serve with salsa.

*Chipotle chilies canned in a spicy tomato sauce, sometimes called adobo, are available at Latin American markets, specialty foods stores and some supermarkets.

2 SERVINGS

Patio Picnic for Two

Tomato and Basil Salad

Southwestern Turkey Burgers
(at left)

**Grilled Corn with
Roasted Garlic Butter**
(page 137; halve recipe)

Beer

Colorado Cowboy Cookies
(page 219)

Maple-glazed Turkey with Dijon Gravy

Maple syrup, marjoram, coriander seeds and lemon peel flavor a do-ahead butter that is spread on the turkey before baking. Grape clusters or steamed baby vegetables, such as carrots and squash, make a pretty garnish for the platter.

MAPLE BUTTER

¾ cup pure maple syrup
3 tablespoons chopped fresh marjoram
¼ cup coriander seeds, coarsely cracked in resealable plastic bag
2 teaspoons grated lemon peel
1 teaspoon cracked black pepper
¾ cup (1½ sticks) unsalted butter, room temperature

TURKEY

1 16- to 18-pound turkey; neck, gizzard and heart reserved
2 cups chopped onions
2 cups chopped celery with leaves
2 cups sliced peeled parsnips (about 5 medium)
1 tablespoon chopped fresh marjoram
3 cups (about) canned low-salt chicken broth

GRAVY

2½ cups (about) canned low-salt chicken broth
3 tablespoons unsalted butter
⅓ cup all purpose flour
1 small bay leaf
2 tablespoons Madeira
1 to 2 tablespoons Dijon mustard
1 teaspoon chopped fresh marjoram

FOR MAPLE BUTTER: Boil maple syrup and 2 tablespoons marjoram in heavy medium saucepan until reduced to 1/2 cup, about 4 minutes. Remove from heat. Mix in 1 tablespoon marjoram, coriander, lemon peel and pepper. Add butter and whisk until well blended. Freeze until butter is firm but still spreadable, stirring occasionally, about 45 minutes. (*Can be prepared 2 days ahead. Cover and refrigerate.*)

FOR TURKEY: Position rack in bottom third of oven; preheat to 375°F. Rinse turkey inside and out; pat dry with paper towels. Place turkey on small rack set in large roasting pan. Starting at neck end, carefully slide hand between skin and breast meat to loosen skin. Rub 1/2 cup maple butter over breast meat under skin. If stuffing turkey, spoon stuffing into neck and main cavities. Tie legs together loosely to hold shape. Rub 1/4 cup maple butter over outside of turkey. Reserve remaining maple butter for gravy. Arrange onions, celery, parsnips and reserved turkey parts around turkey in pan. Sprinkle vegetables with 1 tablespoon marjoram.

Roast turkey 30 minutes. Reduce oven temperature to 350°F. Cover entire turkey (not pan) with foil and roast 1 1/2 hours. Add 2 cups broth to pan; roast turkey 1 1/2 hours. Remove foil. Add 1 cup broth to pan and roast turkey until meat thermometer inserted into thickest part of thigh registers 175°F, basting occasionally with pan juices, about 30 minutes longer if unstuffed or 1 hour longer if stuffed. Transfer turkey to platter; tent with foil and let stand 30 minutes (internal temperature of turkey will increase 5 to 10 degrees). Reserve mixture in pan for gravy.

FOR GRAVY: Strain pan juices into large measuring cup, pressing on solids; discard solids in strainer. Spoon fat from top of pan juices; discard fat. Add enough chicken broth to pan juices in cup to measure 4 1/2 cups. Melt 1/4 cup maple butter and 3 tablespoons butter in heavy large saucepan over medium-high heat. Add flour; whisk constantly until mixture is deep brown, about 8 minutes (mixture will resemble lumpy oatmeal-like paste). Gradually whisk in broth mixture; bring to boil. Add bay leaf and boil until thickened to sauce consistency, whisking occasionally, about 10 minutes. Whisk in Madeira, 1 tablespoon mustard and marjoram. Simmer 2 minutes. Taste, adding more mustard if desired. Season gravy with salt and pepper. Brush turkey with maple butter. Serve turkey with gravy.

10 TO 12 SERVINGS

Celebration Dinner for Twelve

Pear, Onion and Dry Jack Cheese Strudels
(page 14)

Endive Salad with Orange-Ginger Dressing
(page 145)

Maple-glazed Turkey with Dijon Gravy
(opposite; pictured opposite)

Sweet Maple Carrots
(page 133; double recipe)

Mashed Potatoes

Zinfandel

Spice Cake with Blackberry Filling and Cream Cheese Frosting
(page 198)

Roasted Halibut with Tomatoes, Saffron and Cilantro

Saffron adds vivid color as well as unique flavor to this dish. Open a bottle of Chardonnay to accompany the meal.

3 pounds plum tomatoes, cut into 1-inch pieces (about 8 cups)
2 cups red grape tomatoes, halved
1 cup yellow teardrop tomatoes, halved
8 8-ounce halibut fillets (each about 1 inch thick)
½ cup olive oil
3 tablespoons white balsamic vinegar
2 green onions, chopped (white part only)
1 tablespoon chopped fresh cilantro plus cilantro sprigs for garnish
2 tablespoons chopped fresh basil
¼ teaspoon saffron threads

Preheat oven to 450°F. Place all tomatoes in 13x9x2-inch glass baking dish. Sprinkle with salt and pepper; toss to combine. Sprinkle fish with salt and pepper; place atop tomatoes. Whisk oil, vinegar, green onions, chopped cilantro, basil and saffron in small bowl to blend. Season dressing to taste with salt and pepper. Pour dressing evenly over fish. Let stand 10 minutes.

Bake until fish is opaque in center, about 10 minutes. Cool slightly. Place 1 fillet on each of 8 plates. Season tomato mixture to taste with salt and pepper. Top fish with tomato mixture, dividing equally. Garnish with cilantro sprigs. Serve warm.

8 SERVINGS

Sea Bass with Moroccan Salsa

Seafood

3 medium-size red bell peppers
5 tablespoons olive oil
1 teaspoon ground cumin
½ teaspoon ground cinnamon
½ cup chopped pitted Kalamata olives or other brine-cured black olives
½ cup chopped red onion
⅓ cup chopped fresh cilantro
¼ cup golden raisins
3 tablespoons fresh lemon juice
2 tablespoons (packed) chopped fresh mint
2 teaspoons grated orange peel
½ teaspoon (scant) cayenne pepper

6 6-ounce sea bass fillets

Char peppers over gas flame or in broiler until blackened on all sides, turning frequently with tongs. Transfer peppers to medium bowl. Cover with foil; let stand 10 minutes. Peel, seed and chop peppers; return to same bowl. Heat 1 tablespoon oil in heavy small skillet over medium heat. Add cumin and cinnamon; stir until fragrant, about 1 minute. Pour oil mixture over peppers. Mix in olives, next 7 ingredients and 2 tablespoons oil. Season salsa with salt and pepper. *(Can be prepared 2 hours ahead. Cover; let stand at room temperature, tossing occasionally.)*

Preheat broiler. Brush fish all over with remaining 2 tablespoons oil. Sprinkle with salt and pepper. Broil until fish is opaque in center, about 2½ minutes per side. Transfer fish to plates. Spoon salsa over and serve.

6 SERVINGS

Salsa Rhythms

Check any survey of U.S. eating habits, and you'll learn that salsa is our favorite condiment. And we've expanded far beyond the simple tomato and onion blends.

Green salsas based on cooked tomatillos and mild or hot green chilies go particularly well with pork, poultry and seafood dishes. Fans of spices are discovering the pleasures of salsas based solely on roasted fresh or dried chilies, from smoky-hot chipotles to mellow and mildly hot *anchos*. Traditional salsas based on other vegetables, beans and grains are also finding their way onto tables everywhere.

Tropical-style salsas are popular as well. These mix fruits such as mango, papaya, pineapple and kiwi with onions, chilies and fresh herbs such as cilantro. Such sweet, sharp accompaniments are outstanding with grilled seafood, poultry or even red meat.

Red meat's favored condiment in Argentina, *chimichurri*, is also appearing on U.S. menus. A mixture of garlic, onion, parsley, dried crushed red pepper, cayenne pepper and oil, it also makes an excellent dip.

Salsa's blending of assertive flavors can effectively incorporate the signature seasonings of other lands. From the Moroccan salsa at left to mixtures flavored with Japanese rice vinegar or toasted Indian spices, salsa will only continue gaining in popularity.

Cod with Green Pea Coulis and Bacon

This pretty entrée is perfect accompanied by steamed potatoes and vegetables.

4 thick bacon slices, cut into ½-inch pieces
2 tablespoons (¼ stick) butter
¼ cup minced shallots
1 8-ounce bottle clam juice
½ cup dry white wine
1¾ cups frozen petite peas (about 9 ounces), thawed

4 6-ounce cod or sea bass fillets (each about 1 inch thick)
   All purpose flour

Cook bacon in heavy large skillet over medium-high heat until crisp. Using slotted spoon, transfer bacon to paper towels to drain. Pour 2 tablespoons drippings into small bowl (discard any remaining drippings). Melt 1 tablespoon butter with 1 tablespoon drippings in same skillet over medium-high heat. Add shallots; sauté 2 minutes. Add clam juice and wine; boil until slightly thickened, about 5 minutes. Add peas and simmer 1 minute. Puree pea mixture in processor. Season with salt and pepper. *(Can be prepared 2 hours ahead. Set bacon and puree aside at room temperature.)*

Melt remaining 1 tablespoon butter with 1 tablespoon reserved bacon drippings in heavy large skillet over medium-high heat. Sprinkle fish with salt and pepper. Dust lightly with flour. Add fish to skillet; sauté until opaque in center, about 4 minutes per side. Transfer fish to plates. Add pea puree to drippings and bring to boil, stirring frequently. Spoon sauce around fish. Sprinkle with bacon and serve.

4 SERVINGS

Salmon Burgers with Dill Tartar Sauce

- 10 ounces skinless salmon fillet, cut into 1-inch pieces
- 3 tablespoons plus ½ cup purchased tartar sauce
- 2 tablespoons chopped fresh dill
- ¼ teaspoon salt
- ¼ teaspoon ground black pepper

- 1 teaspoon grated lemon peel
- 2 sesame-seed rolls, split
  Red onion slices
- 4 Bibb lettuce leaves

These burgers are easier to handle if they are chilled for one hour before grilling. They would be great with rice salad and cucumber slices.

Place salmon, 3 tablespoons tartar sauce, 1 tablespoon dill, salt and pepper in processor. Using on/off turns, blend until coarsely ground. Form into two ½-inch-thick patties. *(Can be made 6 hours ahead. Cover; chill.)*

Prepare barbecue (medium-high heat). Whisk ½ cup tartar sauce, 1 tablespoon dill and lemon peel in medium bowl to blend. Grill rolls until toasted. Transfer to 2 plates and spread bottom halves generously with sauce. Grill patties until fish is cooked through, about 2 minutes per side. Place burgers atop sauce on rolls. Top each with onion slices, 2 lettuce leaves and top half of roll. Serve, passing remaining sauce separately.

2 SERVINGS

Pan-fried Trout with Bacon

4 bacon slices
5 tablespoons butter
2 8- to 10-ounce trout, boned
  All purpose flour
1 cup thinly sliced green onions
2 tablespoons fresh lemon juice
4 teaspoons drained capers
2 teaspoons chopped fresh tarragon

Cook bacon in large skillet over medium heat until crisp, about 8 minutes. Transfer to paper towels to drain. Crumble bacon. Pour off all but 3 table-spoons drippings from skillet. Add 1 tablespoon butter and stir to melt. Sprinkle fish with salt and pepper. Coat flesh side of fish with flour; shake off excess. Add fish, flesh side down, to skillet. Cook 2 minutes. Turn fish over. Cook until just opaque in center, about 2 minutes longer. Transfer fish to 2 plates. Pour off drippings from skillet; wipe skillet clean. Melt remaining 4 tablespoons butter in same skillet over medium heat. Add all but 2 tablespoons onions; sauté 3 minutes. Stir in bacon, lemon juice, capers and tarragon. Season sauce with salt and pepper. Pour sauce over fish. Sprinkle fish with remaining 2 tablespoons green onions.

2 SERVINGS

Sea Bass with Miso-Mustard Sauce

The miso-mustard sauce is also good on grilled vegetables and chicken.

2 teaspoons water
1 teaspoon prepared Chinese-style hot mustard or Dijon mustard
⅓ cup white miso (fermented soybean paste)*
3 tablespoons rice vinegar
2 tablespoons mirin (sweet Japanese rice wine)*
4 teaspoons sugar
1 teaspoon soy sauce

4 5- to 6-ounce sea bass fillets
8 green onions, trimmed
  Olive oil
  Toasted sesame seeds

Whisk water and mustard in small bowl. Combine next 5 ingredients in small saucepan. Stir over medium heat about 3 minutes. Whisk in mustard mixture. (*Can be prepared 1 day ahead. Rewarm over low heat before using.*)

Prepare barbecue (medium-high heat). Brush fish and green onions with oil. Sprinkle both with salt and pepper. Grill fish until opaque in center, about 4 minutes per side. Grill onions until beginning to brown, about 3 minutes per side. Transfer fish and onions to 4 plates. Spread sauce atop fish. Sprinkle sesame seeds over sauce and serve.

Sold at Japanese markets and in the Asian foods section of some supermarkets.

4 SERVINGS

Fresh Tuna Tacos

- ⅓ cup sour cream
- ¼ cup chopped red onion
- 3 tablespoons chopped cilantro
- 1 teaspoon minced canned chipotle chilies*
- 1 8-ounce ahi tuna steak, cut into ¾-inch pieces
- 1 tablespoon taco seasoning mix
- 1 tablespoon vegetable oil
- 4 taco shells

Serve these tacos with salsa, shredded lettuce, sliced avocado and black olives. Corn and black bean salad finishes the meal—except for the dessert. We recommend spice cake.

Mix first 4 ingredients in small bowl. Place tuna in medium bowl and sprinkle with taco seasoning. Heat oil in heavy medium skillet over medium-high heat. Add tuna; sauté to desired doneness, 3 minutes for medium. Reduce heat to medium-low. Stir in sour cream mixture. Cook just until heated through, stirring frequently, about 2 minutes (do not boil).

Heat taco shells in microwave 20 seconds. Fill taco shells with tuna mixture.

Chipotle chilies canned in a spicy tomato sauce, sometimes called adobo, *are sold at Latin American markets, specialty foods stores and some supermarkets.*

MAKES 4

Roasted Salmon
with Olive-Mustard Butter and Orzo

½   cup (1 stick) butter, room temperature
12   Kalamata olives or other brine-cured black olives, pitted, chopped
1   medium shallot, chopped
1   tablespoon chopped fresh Italian parsley
2   teaspoons Dijon mustard

Olive oil
8   6- to 8-ounce salmon fillets (each about 1¼ to 1½ inches thick)

2½   cups orzo (rice-shaped pasta; about 1¼ pounds)
Whole Kalamata olives (optional)
Fresh Italian parsley sprigs (optional)

Mix first 5 ingredients in processor until well blended but still slightly chunky, occasionally scraping down sides of bowl. Season butter mixture to taste with salt and pepper. Transfer to small bowl. *(Olive-mustard butter can be prepared 2 days ahead. Cover and refrigerate. Soften slightly at room temperature before using.)*

Preheat oven to 400°F. Brush large rimmed baking sheet with olive oil. Arrange salmon fillets on prepared sheet; sprinkle with salt and pepper. Roast salmon just until opaque in center, about 14 minutes.

Meanwhile, cook orzo in large pot of boiling salted water until tender but still firm to bite. Drain; return orzo to same pot. Add half of olive-mustard butter and toss to coat. Divide orzo among 8 plates. Top each with 1 fillet. Place small dollop of olive-mustard butter atop each fillet. Garnish with whole olives and parsley sprigs, if desired, and serve.

8 SERVINGS

Halibut and Red Pepper Skewers with Chili-Lime Sauce

½ cup fresh lime juice

4 tablespoons olive oil

2 tablespoons sugar

3 tablespoons chopped fresh cilantro

1½ teaspoons minced serrano chilies with seeds

1½ pounds 1-inch-thick halibut fillets, cut into 1-inch cubes (about 30 pieces)

1 large red bell pepper, cut into 1-inch triangles (about 30 pieces)

6 green onions, cut into 1-inch lengths (about 30 pieces)

6 12-inch metal skewers

Whisk lime juice, 2 tablespoons oil, sugar, cilantro and chilies in small bowl until sugar dissolves. Let stand 1 hour at room temperature to allow flavors to blend. Season with salt and pepper. *(Chili-lime sauce can be prepared 8 hours ahead. Cover; chill. Bring sauce to room temperature before using.)*

Prepare barbecue (medium-high heat). Alternate halibut pieces, pepper pieces and onion pieces on skewers. Sprinkle with salt and pepper. Drizzle with remaining 2 tablespoons oil. Grill until fish is opaque in center and singed in places, turning occasionally, about 6 minutes. Transfer kebabs to platter. Serve, passing chili-lime sauce separately.

6 SERVINGS

Grilled Shrimp with Roasted Garlic-Herb Sauce

Fish on the Grill for Six

Green Salad with Tortilla Strips and Queso Fresco
(page 140)

Grilled Shrimp with Roasted Garlic-Herb Sauce
(at left; pictured opposite)

Halibut and Red Pepper Skewers with Chili-Lime Sauce
(opposite; pictured opposite)

Steamed Rice

Pinot Blanc

Mocha Ice Cream Sundaes with Coffee-Caramel Sauce
(page 214)

1	quart water
⅓	cup salt
⅓	cup (packed) golden brown sugar
1½	pounds uncooked large shrimp, unpeeled
¼	cup olive oil
2	tablespoons dry white wine
2	garlic cloves, minced
1	tablespoon chopped fresh parsley
¼	teaspoon dried crushed red pepper
	Roasted Garlic-Herb Sauce (see recipe below)

Stir first 3 ingredients in medium bowl until sugar dissolves. Add shrimp. Refrigerate at least 1 hour and up to 3 hours. Drain and rinse shrimp. Using shears, cut shrimp shells down center of back all the way to tail section. Using sharp knife, cut shrimp in their shells along the full length of the back (do not cut all the way through). Remove vein and pull off legs. Open shrimp. Whisk oil and next 4 ingredients in clean medium bowl. Add shrimp and stir; let stand 30 minutes.

Prepare barbecue (medium-high heat). Place shrimp, flesh side down, on grill. Grill shrimp until pink and cooked through, about 2 minutes per side. Transfer shrimp to platter and serve, passing sauce separately.

6 SERVINGS

Roasted Garlic-Herb Sauce

2	heads of garlic, top ¼ inch of each cut off and discarded
1	teaspoon plus ⅔ cup olive oil
1	cup coarsely chopped fresh parsley
4	anchovy fillets, rinsed
2	tablespoons drained capers
2	tablespoons coarsely chopped fresh basil
1	tablespoon grated lemon peel

Preheat oven to 375°F. Place garlic in small glass baking dish. Drizzle with 1 teaspoon oil. Cover dish with foil. Roast until garlic is tender, 1 hour. Cool slightly. Squeeze garlic from skins into bowl. Mash with fork.

Place garlic, parsley and next 4 ingredients in processor. With machine running, slowly blend in ⅔ cup oil. Season sauce with salt and pepper. *(Can be prepared 1 day ahead. Chill. Bring to room temperature before using.)*

MAKES ABOUT 1 CUP

5 tablespoons butter

2 tablespoons olive oil

1 large sweet onion (such as Vidalia or Maui), halved, thickly sliced crosswise

4 garlic cloves, minced

24 2-inch-long asparagus tips

4 ounces sugar snap peas, strings removed

6 fresh thyme sprigs

⅓ cup canned vegetable broth

1 tablespoon fresh lemon juice

1 heart of romaine lettuce, sliced crosswise into 1-inch strips

1 cup frozen peas, thawed

20 sea scallops, side muscles trimmed

4 lemon wedges

Melt 2 tablespoons butter with oil in heavy large pot over medium-low heat. Add onion and sauté until beginning to soften, about 6 minutes. Add garlic and sauté about 30 seconds. Increase heat to medium-high; add asparagus tips, sugar snap peas and thyme sprigs and sauté 2 minutes. Sprinkle with salt and pepper. Add vegetable broth and lemon juice, then lettuce and peas. Cover and cook until lettuce is wilted, stirring frequently, about 2 minutes. Whisk 1 tablespoon butter into ragout. Remove pot from heat.

Sprinkle scallops with salt and pepper. Melt remaining 2 tablespoons butter in heavy large skillet over medium-high heat. Working in batches, add scallops to skillet and sear until brown and just opaque in center, about 2 minutes per side. Divide ragout among 4 bowls. Top with scallops, dividing equally. Garnish each with 1 lemon wedge.

4 SERVINGS

Shrimp Salad with Zucchini and Basil

¼ cup fresh lemon juice
3 tablespoons drained capers
1 shallot, minced
1 tablespoon Dijon mustard
½ teaspoon dried crushed red pepper
½ cup olive oil
½ cup chopped fresh basil

1 pound uncooked large shrimp, peeled, deveined
2 zucchini, cut into ½-inch cubes (about 2 cups)

8 cups mixed baby greens (about 5 ounces)
Freshly grated Parmesan cheese (optional)

Use packaged prewashed mixed baby greens to make this salad in practically no time. A chilled Sauvignon Blanc pairs well with the dish's fresh, bright flavors.

Whisk lemon juice, capers, shallot, mustard and dried red pepper in medium bowl. Whisk in oil, then basil. Season dressing to taste with salt and pepper.

Bring large saucepan of salted water to boil. Add shrimp and cook 1 minute. Add zucchini; continue cooking until shrimp are opaque in center and zucchini is crisp-tender, about 1 minute longer. Drain. Rinse under cold water and cool. Drain well. Transfer to large bowl. Add ⅓ cup dressing and toss to coat. Season to taste with salt and pepper.

Toss greens in large bowl with enough dressing to coat. Divide greens among 4 plates. Arrange shrimp and zucchini atop greens. Serve, passing Parmesan cheese separately if desired.

4 SERVINGS

After parboiling the lobsters, set them aside. Add potatoes and onions; ladle off some of the cooking liquid and reserve. Partially cook vegetables for ten minutes, and follow with a layer of sausages and corn.

For the last layer, clams and parboiled lobsters should be placed on top of the sausages and corn.

HERB AND GARLIC BUTTER

1 cup (2 sticks) butter, room temperature
3 large garlic cloves, finely chopped
1 teaspoon dried oregano
1 teaspoon dried basil

VEGETABLES, SAUSAGES AND SEAFOOD

6 dozen littleneck clams, scrubbed
¼ cup yellow cornmeal

2 celery stalks, cut crosswise in half
6 large fresh parsley sprigs
6 fresh thyme sprigs
2 small dried bay leaves
¼ teaspoon whole black peppercorns
3 1½-pound live lobsters

12 small (about 2-inch-diameter) red-skinned new potatoes, scrubbed
6 small onions, peeled
1½ pounds fully cooked smoked sausages (such as kielbasa or andouille), cut into 6 portions
6 ears of corn, husked

Chopped fresh parsley
Lemon wedges

FOR HERB AND GARLIC BUTTER: Blend all ingredients in bowl. Season butter with salt and pepper. (*Can be made 2 days ahead. Cover; chill.*)

FOR VEGETABLES, SAUSAGES AND SEAFOOD: Place clams and cornmeal (to help purge clams of sand) in very large bowl or pot; fill with enough cold salted water to cover. Set aside at least 30 minutes and up to 1 hour.

Place 12-inch square of cheesecloth on work surface. Place celery, parsley, thyme, bay leaves and peppercorns in center. Roll up cheesecloth and tie with string. Place bouquet garni in large (at least 18-quart) pot. Half-fill pot with cold water and bring to boil over high heat. Add 1 lobster headfirst; cover pot. Boil until lobster is almost cooked through and shell turns bright red, about 8 minutes. Using tongs, transfer lobster to bowl. Repeat with remaining lobsters.

Add potatoes and onions to pot. Ladle off cooking liquid into large bowl, leaving just enough to cover vegetables; reserve liquid in bowl. Bring liquid in pot to boil. Cover; cook potatoes and onions 10 minutes. Layer sausages and corn atop vegetables. Cover pot and cook until potatoes are just tender, about 10 minutes.

Rinse clams thoroughly. Arrange clams atop corn and sausages. Place lobsters on top of clams. Cover pot tightly with lid or, if necessary, cover tightly with overlapping large sheets of foil. Boil until clams open, about 12 minutes. Remove from heat.

Transfer lobsters to work surface, shell side down. Place tip of large knife in center of 1 lobster. Cut lobster lengthwise in half from center to end of head (knife might not cut through shell), then cut lobster in half from center to end of tail. If necessary, use kitchen shears to cut through shell. Repeat with remaining lobsters. Mound clams (discarding any that did not open), lobsters and sausages on large platter; reserve cooking broth in pot. Surround seafood with corn, potatoes and, if desired, onions. Sprinkle vegetables with salt, pepper and parsley. Sprinkle with parsley; garnish with lemon wedges. Cover with foil to keep warm.

Melt seasoned butter in saucepan; divide among 6 ramekins. Discard bouquet garni from pot. Taste broth; season with pepper. Add some of reserved lobster cooking liquid if broth is too salty. Bring broth to boil; divide among 6 soup cups. Serve seasoned butter and broth alongside vegetables, sausages and seafood.

6 SERVINGS

The pot needs to be covered tightly during the final cooking phase. If necessary, use large overlapping sheets of aluminum foil.

To cut the lobsters in half, place them shell side down on a work surface. Insert the tip of a large knife into the center of one lobster. Cut lengthwise from center to end of head, then cut from center to end of tail. If necessary, use kitchen shears to cut through the shell.

Indian Dinner
for Eight

Baby Greens with
Cumin Vinaigrette

Shrimp with Spiced Masala and
Coconut Milk
(at right; pictured opposite)

Steamed Basmati Rice

Naan

Chai

Tropical Lime Torte with
Mango Compote
(page 189; pictured on page 160)

Shrimp with Spiced Masala
and Coconut Milk

MASALA

2	tablespoons vegetable oil
2	cups chopped onions
4	large garlic cloves, minced
1½	teaspoons garam masala*
1½	teaspoons curry powder
1½	teaspoons ground coriander
1	teaspoon turmeric
½	teaspoon cayenne pepper
1	28-ounce can diced tomatoes in juice
1	cup plain whole-milk yogurt

SHRIMP

2	tablespoons vegetable oil
2	pounds uncooked large shrimp, peeled, deveined
1	13½-ounce can unsweetened coconut milk**
½	cup chopped fresh cilantro
¼	cup chopped green onion tops
1½	tablespoons fresh lemon juice

FOR MASALA: Heat oil in large nonstick skillet over medium heat. Add onions; sauté until deep golden, about 20 minutes. Add garlic and all spices; stir 1 minute. Cool to lukewarm. Puree tomatoes with juices and yogurt in processor until almost smooth. Add onion mixture; puree until almost smooth. Season masala to taste with salt and pepper. (*Masala can be prepared 1 day ahead. Cover and refrigerate.*)

FOR SHRIMP: Heat oil in heavy large deep skillet over medium-high heat. Add shrimp and sauté until partially cooked, about 2 minutes. Stir in coconut milk, cilantro, green onions, lemon juice and prepared masala. Simmer until shrimp are opaque in center, about 3 minutes longer. Season to taste with salt and pepper and serve.

A spice mixture available at Indian markets and some specialty foods stores. To substitute, mix 3/4 teaspoon ground cumin with 3/4 teaspoon ground coriander, 1/2 teaspoon freshly ground pepper, 1/2 teaspoon ground cardamom, 1/4 teaspoon ground cloves and 1/4 teaspoon cinnamon. Use 1 1/2 teaspoons of mixture for the recipe.
**Available at Indian, Southeast Asian and Latin American markets and many supermarkets nationwide.*

8 SERVINGS

Root Vegetable Cobbler
with Chive Biscuit Topping

This meatless cobbler is packed with root vegetables and wild mushrooms, and blanketed with a chive biscuit topping. Serve it with a Zinfandel or a dry Riesling.

FILLING

- 3 tablespoons butter
- 1 large onion, chopped
- 1½ pounds white-skinned potatoes, peeled, cut into ½-inch pieces (about 3⅔ cups)
- 1 8- to 9-ounce turnip, peeled, cut into ½-inch pieces
- 1 large carrot, peeled, cut into ½-inch pieces
- 1 ½-ounce package dried porcini mushrooms*
- 1½ teaspoons dried thyme
- ¾ teaspoon ground cumin
- ½ teaspoon ground black pepper
- 1 14½-ounce can vegetable broth
- 1 cup water
- 1 cup whipping cream
- 8 ounces fresh shiitake mushrooms, stemmed, caps diced
- 1 cup frozen peas
- ¼ cup chopped fresh chives
- 1 tablespoon all purpose flour

BISCUIT TOPPING

- 2 cups all purpose flour
- 1 tablespoon baking powder
- 1 teaspoon salt
- ¼ cup chopped fresh chives
- 6 tablespoons chilled unsalted butter, cut into ½-inch pieces
- 2 large eggs
- ½ cup whole milk

FOR FILLING: Melt 2 tablespoons butter in heavy large pot over medium-high heat. Add onion; sauté until deep golden, about 7 minutes. Add next 7 ingredients; stir 1 minute. Add broth and 1 cup water; bring to boil. Reduce heat, cover and simmer until vegetables are almost tender, about 10 minutes. Stir in cream and next 3 ingredients. Season with salt. Bring to simmer. Mix 1 tablespoon butter and flour in small bowl to blend. Stir into vegetable mixture; simmer until mixture thickens slightly, about 5 minutes. Divide among six 2-cup soufflé or baking dishes; set aside. *(Can be prepared 1½ hours ahead. Let stand at room temperature.)*

FOR BISCUIT TOPPING: Preheat oven to 425°F. Sift flour, baking powder and salt into bowl. Stir in chives. Add butter; rub in with fingertips until mixture resembles coarse meal. Add eggs and milk and stir until soft moist

Meatless

dough forms. Turn dough out onto generously floured surface. Knead gently just to combine. Divide dough into 6 equal pieces; pat out each piece to 3½-inch round. Place 1 dough round atop vegetable filling in each dish (some filling will show around edges). Place dishes on large baking sheet. Bake until topping is golden and vegetable mixture is heated through, about 18 minutes. Let stand 5 minutes. Serve hot.

Dried porcinis are available at Italian markets and many supermarkets.

6 SERVINGS

Oven-roasted Spring Vegetables
with Salsa Verde

Serve this flavor-packed entrée by itself or paired with the polenta recipe opposite (pictured below). To save time, a good commercially made *salsa verde* can be substituted.

1 lemon, halved
12 baby artichokes

Nonstick olive oil spray
2 large fennel bulbs, trimmed, each cut lengthwise into 8 wedges
6 slender leeks (white and pale green parts only), root ends trimmed, each leek cut lengthwise in half
18 thick asparagus spears, tough ends trimmed
12 very slender small carrots, peeled
Olive oil
Salsa Verde (see recipe opposite)

Squeeze juice from lemon halves into large bowl; add lemon halves. Fill bowl with water. Trim stem of 1 artichoke. Starting at base, bend leaves back and snap off where leaves break naturally, continuing until all tough outer leaves have been removed. Using small sharp knife, trim outside of base until smooth and no dark green areas remain. Cut artichoke lengthwise in half. Using tip of knife, remove any purple-tipped leaves from center. Add artichoke to lemon water. Repeat with remaining artichokes. Bring large pot of salted water to boil. Drain artichokes. Add to boiling water; cook until just tender, about 8 minutes. Drain artichokes; set aside. *(Can be prepared 1 day ahead; cover and refrigerate.)*

Preheat oven to 375°F. Spray 3 large rimmed baking sheets with nonstick spray. Arrange artichoke halves, fennel and leeks in single layer on 2 prepared sheets. Arrange asparagus and carrots in single layer on third sheet. Brush vegetables with oil. Sprinkle with salt and pepper. Roast vegetables until tender, turning over halfway through, about 35 minutes total for artichokes, fennel and leeks and 20 minutes total for asparagus and carrots. Divide vegetables among 6 plates. Drizzle Salsa Verde over.

6 SERVINGS

Salsa Verde

3 cups (loosely packed) fresh Italian parsley leaves (from 1 very large bunch)
½ cup extra-virgin olive oil
3 green onions, sliced
3 tablespoons fresh lemon juice
3 garlic cloves, peeled
2 drained anchovy fillets (optional)
1 tablespoon drained capers
1 tablespoon Dijon mustard
1½ teaspoons grated lemon peel

Combine all ingredients in processor. Using on/off turns, process to coarse paste. Season with salt and pepper. (*Can be made 1 day ahead. Cover; chill.*)

MAKES ABOUT 1½ CUPS

Creamy Baked Polenta with Herbs and Green Onions

6 cups water
1½ cups polenta (coarse cornmeal) or yellow cornmeal
2 teaspoons salt
¼ teaspoon ground black pepper

2 tablespoons (¼ stick) butter
4 green onions, thinly sliced
3 tablespoons minced fresh Italian parsley
1½ teaspoons minced fresh thyme
¼ cup whipping cream

¾ cup grated dry Jack cheese or freshly grated Parmesan cheese
1 teaspoon grated lemon peel

Preheat oven to 350°F. Pour 6 cups water into 13x9x2-inch glass baking dish. Whisk polenta, salt and pepper into water. Bake uncovered 40 minutes.

Meanwhile, melt butter in small skillet over medium heat. Add green onions and sauté 2 minutes. Stir in parsley and thyme, then cream. Season with salt and pepper. Remove from heat.

Stir polenta to blend. Stir green onion mixture, cheese and lemon peel into polenta. Continue to bake uncovered until polenta is creamy and liquid is completely absorbed, about 10 minutes longer. Let stand 5 minutes; serve.

6 SERVINGS

**Rustic Lunch
for Six**

Blood Orange and
Blue Cheese Salad
(*page 150*)

**Creamy Baked Polenta with
Herbs and Green Onions**
(*at left; pictured opposite*)

Crushed-Mint Lemonade
(*page 35*)

Ciabatta

Fruit Turnovers

Rice Perfect

Even some of the most experienced, self-assured cooks go back to their reference books—or at least check label instructions—when cooking rice. That's because there are as many different methods for cooking rice, from saucepans to microwaves to electric cookers, as there are different types of rice available.

The following instructions will yield about four half-cup servings of fluffy long-grain white rice, the kind most commonly cooked in American kitchens: Place 1¾ cups cold water and 1 cup rice in a saucepan; if you like, add ¼ to ½ teaspoon salt. Bring to a boil over high heat. Stir, reduce heat to very low, cover securely and cook until rice is tender and no excess liquid remains, about 15 to 20 minutes. Remove rice from heat and let stand, covered, for about 10 minutes before serving.

For stickier short- and medium-grain rice, decrease the water to 1½ cups for 1 cup uncooked rice and cook for the same amount of time. For short-grain brown rice, increase the water to 2 cups and the cooking time to 35 to 45 minutes. For the unrelated, nutty-tasting grain known as wild rice, rinse first. Use 3 cups water, simmer covered for about 1 hour, and drain off any remaining liquid.

Yellow Rice Salad with Roasted Peppers and Spicy Black Beans

4	teaspoons ground cumin
¼	cup fresh lime juice
2½	tablespoons vegetable oil
½	teaspoon turmeric
2	cups water
1	cup basmati rice
1	teaspoon salt
½	cup thinly sliced green onions
1	15- to 16-ounce can black beans, rinsed, drained
½	cup chopped roasted red peppers from jar
½	cup chopped green bell pepper
⅓	cup chopped fresh cilantro
1½	teaspoons minced canned chipotle chilies*

Stir 3 teaspoons cumin in small dry skillet over medium heat just until fragrant, about 1 minute. Remove from heat. Whisk lime juice and oil into skillet.

Stir turmeric and 1 teaspoon cumin in medium saucepan over medium heat until fragrant, 1 minute. Add water, rice and salt; bring to boil. Reduce heat to low; cover. Simmer until water is absorbed, 15 minutes. Cool rice. Mix onions and half of dressing into rice. Season with salt and pepper.

Combine last 5 ingredients with remaining dressing. Toss to coat. Season with salt and pepper. Mound beans in center of platter. Surround with rice.

Chipotle chilies canned in a spicy tomato sauce, sometimes called adobo, are available at Latin American markets, specialty foods stores and some supermarkets.

4 SERVINGS

102

Toasted Barley and Asparagus "Risotto"

Lighter Luncheon for Four

Greens with
Balsamic Vinaigrette

Toasted Barley and
Asparagus "Risotto"
(at left)

Pinot Grigio

Triple-Chocolate Biscotti
(page 218)

12 ounces asparagus, trimmed, cut into ¾-inch pieces

2 cups pearl barley

3 tablespoons butter

1 cup finely chopped onion

3 large garlic cloves, finely chopped

8½ cups (about) canned vegetable broth

2 cups drained canned diced tomatoes in juice

½ cup freshly grated Parmesan cheese

½ cup chopped arugula or 3 tablespoons chopped fresh parsley

2 teaspoons grated lemon peel

Cook asparagus in pot of boiling salted water until crisp-tender, about 3 minutes. Drain. Transfer to bowl of ice water to cool. Drain again. *(Can be prepared 1 day ahead. Cover and refrigerate.)*

Stir barley in heavy large saucepan over medium heat until lightly toasted, about 5 minutes. Transfer barley to bowl. Melt butter in same saucepan over medium heat. Add onion and garlic; sauté until tender, about 5 minutes. Add barley and stir to coat. Add 2 cups broth; reduce heat to medium-low and simmer until liquid is absorbed, stirring frequently, about 7 minutes. Mix in 2½ cups broth and simmer until absorbed, stirring frequently. Add 3 cups broth and simmer until barley is tender and creamy but still slightly firm to bite, stirring frequently and adding more broth if mixture is dry, about 45 minutes. Add tomatoes and asparagus; stir until heated through, about 3 minutes. Mix in cheese, arugula and lemon peel. Season with salt and pepper.

4 SERVINGS

Asian Vegetables with Tofu and Coconut Milk

This flavorful meatless dish makes a light-but-filling main course for two people as suggested here—or it can become a side dish for four. If you are serving it as an entrée, add steamed rice to round out the meal.

8 small broccoli florets
8 small cauliflower florets
1 tablespoon oriental sesame oil
2 large garlic cloves, minced
12 pieces canned baby corn, drained
8 snow peas, strings removed
6 large shiitake mushrooms (about 4 ounces), stemmed, caps sliced
1 small Chinese or Japanese eggplant, quartered lengthwise, cut crosswise into 1-inch pieces
¾ cup canned unsweetened coconut milk*
2 tablespoons soy sauce
1 tablespoon oyster sauce* or vegetarian oyster sauce*
1 2-inch square baked teriyaki-seasoned tofu, cut into 1x½x¼-inch pieces
1 baby bok choy, quartered lengthwise
1 green onion, cut into 1-inch pieces

Cook broccoli and cauliflower in pot of boiling salted water 1 minute. Drain and set aside. Heat oil in large nonstick skillet over medium-high heat. Add garlic and stir 30 seconds. Add broccoli, cauliflower, corn, snow peas, mushrooms and eggplant. Cover and cook until vegetables are almost tender, stirring occasionally, about 4 minutes. Mix in coconut milk, soy sauce and oyster sauce. Add tofu, bok choy and green onion. Cover; cook vegetables until just tender and coated with sauce, about 2 minutes longer. Sprinkle with pepper. Transfer vegetables to large bowl and serve.

Available at Asian markets and in the Asian foods section of most supermarkets.

2 SERVINGS

Greek Salad Pita Sandwiches

The classic combination of olives, tomatoes, cucumber and feta makes a delicious— and easy—salad filling.

¼ cup extra-virgin olive oil
1 tablespoon fresh lemon juice
2 tablespoons chopped pitted Kalamata olives or other brine-cured black olives
1 teaspoon dried oregano
3 cups (loosely packed) thinly sliced romaine lettuce
2 cups diced seeded tomatoes
1 cucumber, peeled, halved, seeded, cut into ¼-inch cubes
1 cup crumbled feta cheese (about 4 ounces)
6 6-inch pita breads, top 1½ inches trimmed

Whisk first 4 ingredients in large bowl to blend. Add next 4 ingredients and toss to combine. Season salad with salt and pepper. Carefully open pita breads at cut end. Fill each with salad and serve.

6 SERVINGS

Rolled Mushroom Blini with Parmesan

1½ tablespoons butter
12 ounces assorted wild mushrooms (such as crimini, oyster and stemmed shiitake), sliced
1 large shallot, chopped
⅓ cup canned vegetable broth
⅔ cup whipping cream
¼ cup grated Parmesan cheese

4 5- to 6-inch purchased crepes

Melt butter in medium skillet over medium heat. Add mushrooms and shallot; sauté until tender, about 5 minutes. Add broth. Simmer until liquid evaporates, about 30 seconds. Add cream. Simmer until thickened, about 1 minute. Remove from heat. Stir in Parmesan. Season mushroom mixture with salt and pepper.

Meanwhile, wrap crepes in plastic wrap. Heat in microwave until warm, about 15 seconds. Divide crepes between 2 plates. Spoon 1/6 of mushrooms and sauce down center of each crepe. Roll up crepes. Top with remaining mushrooms and sauce and serve.

2 SERVINGS

Grilled Fontina, Mushroom and Arugula Sandwiches

6	tablespoons (about) olive oil
1	teaspoon minced fresh rosemary
4	very large portobello mushrooms, stemmed, dark gills removed, caps thinly sliced
8	½-inch-thick slices country white bread (each about 3x6 inches)
	Dijon mustard (optional)
8	ounces Fontina cheese, thinly sliced
2	bunches arugula or 1 bunch trimmed watercress

Heat 4 tablespoons oil in heavy large skillet over medium-high heat. Add rosemary and stir 30 seconds. Add mushrooms. Cover skillet and cook until mushrooms are tender, stirring often, about 8 minutes. Season mushrooms to taste with salt and pepper; transfer to plate. Wipe out skillet.

Arrange 4 bread slices on work surface; spread with mustard, if desired. Top bread slices with cheese, then mushrooms and arugula, dividing equally. Top each with bread slice; press to compact. Brush tops lightly with oil.

Heat reserved skillet over medium heat. Place sandwiches, oiled side down, in skillet. Brush tops lightly with oil. Cover and cook until golden on bottom, occasionally pressing with spatula, about 5 minutes. Turn sandwiches over. Cover and cook until golden on bottom and cheese is melted, about 5 minutes longer. Transfer sandwiches to plates; cut in half and serve.

4 SERVINGS

Farmers' Market Menu for Four

Chilled Cream of Zucchini Soup with Mussels and Fresh Mint
(page 26)

Grilled Fontina, Mushroom and Arugula Sandwiches
(at left)

Veggie Chips

Zinfandel

Cantaloupe Granita
(page 215)

Portobello Panache

Not so long ago, no one gave a second glance to common cultivated brown-skinned mushrooms that had grown beyond the attractive button size to a diameter as wide as six inches. It wasn't widely known that, in their maturity, they lost moisture and gained a corresponding rich, meaty flavor and texture.

Then, in the 1980s, some clever marketers began to call such dark, oversize mushrooms by the romantic and Italian-sounding name *portobello*. (The smaller form is the *crimini*, a cousin to the familiar snow-white button mushroom.) Suddenly, portobello mushrooms were popular. Today they appear on chic restaurant menus and in well-stocked supermarket produce departments.

It's a good thing, too, because portobello mushrooms are delicious and easy to prepare. First, brush off any dirt and remove their tough stems. Grill or broil the caps whole to eat like a burger patty in sandwiches, or serve as an elegant appetizer. Or scrape out the gills, which can discolor other ingredients, then slice and sauté them for pasta sauces or stir-fries.

Broiled Portobellos Topped with Creamy Scrambled Eggs

    6 4- to 5-inch-diameter portobello mushrooms
       Olive oil
    3 garlic cloves, minced

   12 large eggs
    4 tablespoons grated Parmesan cheese
 1½ teaspoons chopped fresh rosemary
 ¾ teaspoon salt
 ½ teaspoon ground black pepper
    6 tablespoons (¾ stick) butter

Preheat broiler. Line large baking sheet with foil. Remove and discard mushroom stems. Scoop out and discard tough inside centers where mushroom stems were attached. Brush both sides of mushrooms generously with olive oil. Place mushrooms, dark gill side up, on prepared baking sheet. Sprinkle mushrooms with minced garlic, then sprinkle generously with salt and pepper. Broil mushrooms about 5 inches from heat source until beginning to soften, about 5 minutes. Turn mushrooms over; broil until tender when pierced with knife, about 7 minutes longer. *(Can be prepared 2 hours ahead. Let stand at room temperature. Before continuing, rewarm in 350°F oven until heated through, about 10 minutes.)*

Whisk eggs, 2 tablespoons grated Parmesan cheese, rosemary, salt and pepper in large bowl to blend. Melt 5 tablespoons butter in heavy large skillet over medium-low heat. Add eggs to skillet and stir gently in circular motion with wooden spoon or heat-resistant rubber spatula, releasing cooked eggs from bottom of skillet and allowing uncooked portion of eggs to flow underneath. Cook until eggs are set but still soft, about 4 minutes total. Dot with remaining 1 tablespoon butter.

Arrange warm portobello mushrooms, gill side up, on plates. Top with eggs, dividing equally. Sprinkle with remaining 2 tablespoons grated Parmesan cheese, dividing equally, and serve.

6 SERVINGS

Bulgur Pilaf with Roasted Tomatoes, Onions and Garbanzo Beans

2 pounds tomatoes, quartered

1 large onion, cut into ½-inch-thick wedges

2 tablespoons olive oil

1 15-ounce can garbanzo beans (chickpeas), drained

4 garlic cloves, crushed

2½ cups water

2 cups bulgur*

4 tablespoons chopped fresh parsley

2 tablespoons chopped fresh dill

1 tablespoon fresh lemon juice

This hearty pilaf, which combines cracked wheat, tomatoes and garbanzos with lemon and fresh dill, is also a great side dish for eight.

Preheat oven to 400°F. Spread tomatoes and onion in large roasting pan. Drizzle with oil. Sprinkle with salt and pepper. Roast 30 minutes, stirring occasionally. Stir in garbanzo beans and garlic. Roast until onion is golden, stirring occasionally, about 25 minutes longer. Remove pan from oven. Add 2½ cups water to pan and stir, scraping up browned bits.

Transfer vegetable mixture to large saucepan. Bring to boil. Stir in bulgur. Reduce heat to low, cover and simmer until bulgur is tender and liquid is absorbed, about 10 minutes. Stir 3 tablespoons parsley, 1½ tablespoons dill and lemon juice into pilaf. Season with salt and pepper. Transfer to bowl. Sprinkle pilaf with remaining 1 tablespoon parsley and ½ tablespoon dill.

Also called cracked wheat, bulgur is available at natural foods stores and many supermarkets nationwide.

4 SERVINGS

Corn, Cheese and Chili Tamales
with Tomatillo-Avocado Salsa

Poblano **chilies (fresh green chilies, also called** *pasillas*)**, tomatillos (green tomato-like fruits), dried corn husks and Masa Harina are found at many supermarkets and Latin American markets.**

Spread the tamale dough in the center of a softened corn husk. Top the dough with roasted *poblano* chilies and cheese.

Press the dough into the shape of a log, enclosing the chilies and cheese; then fold one long side of the husk over and roll up.

TOMATILLO-AVOCADO SALSA
- 12 tomatillos, husked, rinsed well
- 1 small onion, quartered
- 6 large garlic cloves, peeled
- 2 to 3 serrano chilies, stemmed
- 2 ripe avocados, peeled, diced
- ½ cup chopped fresh cilantro
- 2 tablespoons fresh lime juice

TAMALES
- 1 6-ounce package dried corn husks
- 1 pound large poblano chilies

- 2 cups Masa Harina (corn tortilla mix)
- 6 tablespoons (¾ stick) unsalted butter, room temperature
- 3 tablespoons sugar
- 2¼ teaspoons salt
- ½ cup canned vegetable broth
- 5 cups frozen baby white corn kernels (about 25 ounces), thawed
- 3 cups (packed) coarsely grated sharp cheddar cheese
- 1 teaspoon baking powder
- ⅛ teaspoon ground black pepper

FOR TOMATILLO-AVOCADO SALSA: Cook first 4 ingredients in heavy large skillet over high heat until charred in spots but still firm, turning occasionally, about 5 minutes. Transfer to processor; using on/off turns, chop coarsely. Add all remaining ingredients. Blend to coarse puree. Season with salt and pepper. (*Can be prepared 1 day ahead. Cover; chill.*)

FOR TAMALES: Selecting the largest and cleanest husks, place half of husks in large bowl; fill bowl with warm water. Weigh husks down with plate; soak husks until soft, separating occasionally, about 2 hours. Form 36 ties by tearing several husks into ½-inch-wide strips.

Char chilies directly over gas flame or under broiler until blackened on all sides. Place in medium bowl; cover tightly with plastic. Let stand 10 minutes. Peel, seed and chop chilies.

To make dough, blend Masa Harina, butter, sugar and 1 teaspoon salt in processor until coarse meal forms. Add broth and blend in (mixture will be crumbly). Transfer masa mixture to large bowl. Blend 2½ cups corn, 1 cup cheese, baking powder, pepper and 1¼ teaspoons salt in processor until coarse puree forms. Stir puree, then 2½ cups corn into masa.

For each tamale, open 1 large softened husk. Place ⅓ cup tamale dough in center of husk. Make depression in center of dough; fill with 1 tablespoon chilies, then 1 tablespoon cheese. Using moistened fingertips, press dough over filling to cover; shape filled dough into 3-inch-long log parallel to 1 long edge of husk. Fold 1 long side of husk over filling and roll up to enclose. Tie ends of filled husks tightly with husk strips.

Add enough water to large pot containing steamer insert to reach bottom of insert. Layer tamales in steamer insert. Bring water to boil; cover pot. Steam until tamales are firm, removing insert and adding boiling water to pot to maintain water level as needed, about 1 hour. *(Can be prepared 1 day ahead. Cool slightly. Refrigerate. Before serving, steam 45 minutes to heat through.)* Serve tamales in husks with salsa.

MAKES 18

Use strips of softened corn husk to tie off the ends of each tamale.

Layer the tamales on their sides in the basket insert of a large pot, and steam them until the filling is firm, about one hour.

Succotash and Goat Cheese Quiche

1 refrigerated pie crust (half of 15-ounce package), softened at room
   temperature 15 minutes

3 large eggs
1 cup reduced-fat (2%) milk
½ teaspoon salt
¼ teaspoon ground black pepper
¾ cup frozen lima beans, thawed
½ cup frozen white corn kernels, thawed, drained
½ cup chopped seeded tomatoes
2 tablespoons chopped fresh basil
2 teaspoons chopped fresh oregano
1 garlic clove, minced
¾ cup crumbled soft fresh goat cheese (such as Montrachet)

Preheat oven to 450°F. Line 9-inch-diameter glass pie dish with crust as directed on package for a 1-crust filled pie. Bake until set, about 9 minutes. Cool. Reduce oven temperature to 400°F.

Whisk eggs, milk, salt and pepper in large bowl. Stir in all remaining ingredients. Pour into cooled crust. Bake until golden, puffed and set in center, about 35 minutes. Cool slightly. Serve warm.

8 SERVINGS

Hominy Quesadillas with Tropical Salsa

- 1 cup finely chopped peeled cored pineapple
- 1 cup diced peeled pitted mango
- ½ cup chopped red onion
- ¼ cup chopped fresh cilantro
- 1 jalapeño chili, seeded, chopped
- 8 5- to 6-inch-diameter corn tortillas
- 2 cups (packed) grated hot pepper Monterey Jack cheese (about 8 ounces)
- ¾ cup crumbled feta cheese (about 3 ounces)
- 1 cup drained golden hominy (from 15-ounce can)
- 3 tablespoons (or more) vegetable oil

Stir first 5 ingredients in medium bowl. Season salsa with salt and pepper. Cook tortillas over flame until blackened in spots, 30 seconds per side. Transfer to work surface; cool. Sprinkle 4 tortillas with cheeses and hominy, dividing equally; top with remaining tortillas. Heat 1½ tablespoons oil in each of 2 heavy large skillets over medium heat. Place 2 quesadillas in each skillet. Cook until bottoms are crisp and brown, pressing occasionally with spatula, about 2 minutes. Turn over. Cook until bottoms are brown and cheeses melt, adding more oil as needed, 2 minutes. Cut into quarters. Serve with salsa.

4 SERVINGS

Seared Sesame Tofu with Asian Salad

- ⅔ cup chopped green onions
- ⅔ cup thinly sliced yellow bell pepper
- ⅔ cup mung bean sprouts
- ¼ cup sesame seeds
- 10 ounces extra-firm tofu, cut in about six ½-inch-thick slices, patted dry
- 4 tablespoons roasted garlic oil
- 1½ tablespoons minced peeled fresh ginger
- ¼ cup rice vinegar

Mix green onions, bell pepper and sprouts in bowl. Mound vegetables on 2 plates. Place sesame seeds on small plate. Dredge tofu slices in sesame seeds to coat on all sides. Heat 2 tablespoons oil in heavy medium skillet over medium heat. Add tofu and cook until golden brown, 3 minutes per side. Divide tofu between 2 plates, leaning tofu against vegetable mounds. Add remaining oil to skillet. Add ginger; sauté 1 minute. Add vinegar; bring to boil. Remove from heat. Drizzle tofu and vegetables with pan sauce.

2 SERVINGS

Goat Cheese-Arugula Ravioli
with Tomato-Pancetta Butter

Lightly brushing egg white over the wrapper does two things: It provides a moisture barrier so that the filling doesn't soften the pasta. And it ensures that the ravioli stay sealed while they are cooking.

Form a triangle by folding one corner of the wrapper over the filling to the opposite corner; then press the edges firmly to seal the ravioli.

Pasta & Pizza

RAVIOLI

- 2 tablespoons olive oil
- 3 large shallots, minced
- 8 ounces arugula, chopped (about 8 cups)
- 6 ounces soft fresh goat cheese (such as Montrachet), crumbled
- ½ cup (about 1½ ounces) freshly grated Parmesan cheese

  Nonstick vegetable oil spray
- 42 (about) wonton wrappers (from one 12-ounce package)
- 2 large egg whites, whisked just until foamy

TOMATO-PANCETTA BUTTER

- 6 ounces thinly sliced pancetta* or bacon, coarsely chopped
- ¼ cup (½ stick) butter, plus 5 tablespoons butter, melted
- 6 large plum tomatoes, quartered, seeds and membranes discarded, tomatoes diced
- 1 teaspoon chopped fresh thyme

- 12 fresh basil leaves
  Fresh thyme sprigs

FOR RAVIOLI: Heat oil in heavy large skillet over medium heat. Add shallots; sauté 10 minutes. Add arugula; toss until wilted but still bright green, about 3 minutes. Transfer arugula mixture to large bowl and cool. Mix in goat cheese and Parmesan cheese. Season filling with salt and pepper.

Line 2 baking sheets with heavy-duty foil; spray foil with nonstick spray. Place 4 wonton wrappers on work surface; cover remaining wrappers with plastic to prevent drying. Lightly brush entire surface of each wrapper with egg white. Spoon 1 generous teaspoon filling into center of each wrapper. Fold wrappers diagonally in half, forming triangles. Press edges firmly to seal. Arrange ravioli on prepared sheets. Repeat with remaining wrappers and filling. (*Can be prepared ahead. Cover with plastic and chill up to 1 day; or cover with plastic, then heavy-duty foil, and freeze up to 1 week. If frozen, do not thaw before cooking.*)

FOR TOMATO-PANCETTA BUTTER: Cook pancetta in large skillet over medium-high heat until crisp. Using slotted spoon, transfer to paper towel to drain. Pour off all but 1 tablespoon drippings from skillet. Add ¼ cup butter to skillet; melt over medium-high heat. Add tomatoes and chopped thyme; sauté until tomatoes are tender, 5 minutes. Season with salt and pepper. (*Can be prepared 2 hours ahead. Let stand at room temperature.*)

Place 5 tablespoons melted butter in large bowl. Cook half of ravioli in large pot of boiling salted water until just tender, about 4 minutes for fresh or 5 minutes for frozen. Using large strainer, transfer to colander and drain; place in bowl with butter and toss to coat. Cover to keep warm. Cook remaining ravioli in same pot of boiling water. Drain and add to bowl of buttered ravioli. Toss gently to coat. Divide ravioli among bowls. Rewarm tomato butter over medium heat. Add reserved pancetta and basil; sauté 1 minute. Spoon sauce over ravioli; garnish with thyme sprigs.

Pancetta, Italian bacon cured in salt, is available at Italian markets and in the deli case at many supermarkets.

4 TO 6 SERVINGS

Only the firm tomato shell is used for the pancetta butter; use a small, sharp knife to cut away the flesh and seeds.

Using a large strainer to pull several ravioli out of the water at once ensures that they come out more quickly and don't overcook.

Roasted Vegetable and Prosciutto Lasagna with Alfredo Sauce

²/₃ cup purchased Alfredo sauce
2 ounces thinly sliced prosciutto, cut into ½-inch pieces
2 tablespoons chopped fresh basil
1½ cups canned diced tomatoes with Italian seasonings, undrained
4 (about) no-boil lasagna noodles from one 8-ounce package
1⅓ cups mixed roasted vegetables from deli (such as eggplant, squash and bell peppers)

Stir Alfredo sauce, prosciutto and basil in small bowl to blend. Spread 2 tablespoons Alfredo sauce mixture in bottom of two 1½-cup oval-shaped gratin dishes or two 2-cup soufflé dishes. Top each with ¼ cup tomatoes with juices. Place 1 noodle in each dish, breaking into pieces to fit. Spread each with 2 tablespoons sauce mixture, then ¼ cup tomatoes with juices. Top each with ⅔ cup roasted vegetables. Sprinkle with salt and pepper. Make another layer of noodles, breaking to fit. Top with remaining sauce mixture, dividing equally. Top each with ¼ cup tomatoes with juices.

Cover dishes tightly with plastic wrap. Microwave on high until noodles are tender but still firm to bite, about 10 minutes. Uncover lasagna and let stand 5 minutes before serving.

2 SERVINGS

Creamy Fettuccine with Asparagus, Mushrooms and Peas

8	ounces thin asparagus, trimmed, cut into ½-inch lengths
¼	cup (½ stick) unsalted butter
4	ounces thinly sliced prosciutto, cut into ¼-inch strips
8	ounces crimini mushrooms, sliced
1	cup frozen petite peas, thawed
1	cup whipping cream
16	cherry tomatoes, halved
1	pound fettuccine
⅔	cup grated Parmesan cheese (about 2 ounces)
¼	cup chopped fresh chives

Cook asparagus in large pot of boiling salted water until crisp-tender, 3 minutes. Using slotted spoon, transfer to bowl; set aside. Reserve water in pot.

Melt butter in large skillet over medium-low heat. Add prosciutto and stir 1 minute. Add mushrooms and sauté until golden, about 3 minutes. Add asparagus, peas and cream and simmer until cream is reduced by ⅓, about 2 minutes. Turn off heat. Mix in cherry tomatoes.

Bring reserved water in pot to boil. Add pasta and cook until tender but still firm to bite, stirring occasionally. Drain. Add pasta to skillet with sauce and toss over low heat to coat. Season with salt and pepper. Remove from heat. Stir in cheese. Transfer to bowl; sprinkle with chives and serve.

6 SERVINGS

Mediterranean Evening for Six

Tapenade

Crusty Bread

Creamy Fettuccine with Asparagus, Mushrooms and Peas
(at left)

Greens with Red Wine Vinaigrette

Chardonnay

Whipped Ricotta with Honey and Mixed Berries
(page 184)

Family Supper for Six

Tossed Salad

Classic Spaghetti and Meatballs
(at right)

Breadsticks

Fruit Juice

Chocolate Chip Ice Cream

Classic Spaghetti and Meatballs

3 ¾-inch-thick Italian bread slices (each 3x5 inches) with crusts
  Milk
1 pound ground sirloin
2 tablespoons (packed) grated Parmesan cheese
1 large egg
1 tablespoon minced fresh Italian parsley
1 large garlic clove, minced
1 teaspoon salt
½ teaspoon ground black pepper

2 tablespoons olive oil
  Tomato-Sausage Sauce (see recipe below)

1 pound freshly cooked spaghetti
  Additional grated Parmesan cheese

Place bread in medium bowl; cover with milk. Let stand until bread is soft, about 10 minutes. Place ground sirloin in large bowl. Mix in 2 tablespoons Parmesan cheese and next 5 ingredients. Squeeze bread almost dry; discard milk. Blend bread into meat mixture. Shape mixture into 24 meatballs, using 1 rounded tablespoonful for each.

Heat oil in heavy large skillet over medium heat. Add meatballs; sauté until brown and cooked through, turning often, about 15 minutes. Add meatballs and drippings in skillet to pot of Tomato-Sausage Sauce. Simmer to blend flavors, about 10 minutes.

Place pasta in large bowl. Add 1½ cups sauce and toss to coat. Top with meatballs and remaining sauce. Serve with additional Parmesan cheese.

4 TO 6 SERVINGS

Tomato-Sausage Sauce

6 tablespoons olive oil
4 Italian spicy sausages, pierced several times with toothpick
1 large onion, finely chopped
4 large garlic cloves, minced
1½ 28-ounce cans crushed tomatoes with added puree
¼ cup chopped fresh Italian parsley
2 small bay leaves
2 teaspoons dried basil
2 teaspoons dried oregano

Heat oil in large pot over medium-high heat. Add sausages, onion and garlic; sauté until onion begins to color, about 10 minutes. Add crushed tomatoes and herbs; bring sauce to boil. Reduce heat to medium-low, cover and simmer until flavors blend and sausages are cooked through, stirring often, about 30 minutes. Season with salt and pepper. Slice sausages thinly, if desired.

MAKES ABOUT 5 CUPS

Linguine with Shrimp and Plum Tomatoes

2	pounds uncooked large shrimp, peeled, deveined, tails left intact
10	tablespoons extra-virgin olive oil
1	pound assorted wild mushrooms (such as crimini, baby portobello and stemmed shiitake), sliced
4	pounds plum tomatoes, seeded, chopped (about 7½ cups)
1½	cups chopped fresh basil
1½	cups plus 2 tablespoons chopped fresh parsley
6	garlic cloves, minced
½	teaspoon dried crushed red pepper (optional)
1	pound feta cheese, crumbled (about 2½ cups)
2	cups grated Parmesan cheese
1½	pounds linguine

Place shrimp in medium bowl; sprinkle with salt and pepper. Heat 3 tablespoons oil in heavy large skillet over medium-high heat. Add shrimp; sauté until cooked through, about 3 minutes. Using slotted spoon, transfer to plate; cover. Add 4 tablespoons oil to same skillet. Add mushrooms; sauté until tender, about 8 minutes. Add tomatoes, basil, 1½ cups parsley, garlic and dried red pepper if desired; stir until heated through. Mix in both cheeses.

Meanwhile, cook linguine in large pot of boiling salted water until tender but still firm to bite. Drain. Return to pot. Add 3 tablespoons oil; toss. Add tomato mixture to pasta; toss. Season with salt and pepper. Transfer linguine to bowl. Top with shrimp and 2 tablespoons parsley.

8 SERVINGS

Lighter Lasagna

1 tablespoon extra-virgin olive oil
½ cup finely chopped onion
2 garlic cloves, minced
2 pounds chopped plum tomatoes (about 4 cups)
⅓ cup plus 2 tablespoons chopped fresh basil

1 cup low-fat ricotta cheese
¼ cup (packed) grated low-fat mozzarella cheese

8 freshly cooked lasagna noodles, cut crosswise in half
¼ cup freshly grated Parmesan cheese

Heat oil in large nonstick skillet over medium heat. Add onion and garlic; sauté 3 minutes. Add tomatoes with any juices; simmer until slightly thickened, about 10 minutes. Stir in ⅓ cup basil. Season with salt and pepper.

Stir ricotta cheese in small saucepan over medium-low heat until just heated through. Add mozzarella cheese; stir just until melted, about 1 minute. Season to taste with pepper.

Spoon ¼ cup tomato sauce into bottom of each of 4 shallow bowls. Place 2 hot lasagna noodle halves side by side atop sauce in each bowl. Top with ¼ of cheese mixture, then with 2 more noodle halves. Divide remaining sauce among bowls. Sprinkle with Parmesan cheese and remaining 2 tablespoons basil; serve immediately.

4 SERVINGS

Orecchiette with Rabbit, Tomato and Basil Sauce

5	tablespoons extra-virgin olive oil
1	large onion, chopped
2	garlic cloves, minced
1	2¾- to 3-pound rabbit, cut into pieces, meat finely chopped, or 1 pound finely chopped skinless boneless chicken thigh meat
1	cup dry white wine
1	pound plum tomatoes, chopped
1	28-ounce can crushed tomatoes with added puree
1½	cups chopped fresh basil (from about 3 large bunches)
¼	teaspoon dried crushed red pepper
1	pound orecchiette (little ear-shaped pasta)
	Freshly grated Parmesan cheese

This hearty entrée is made with rabbit, which may be found in the frozen foods section of some supermarkets—or ordered from your butcher. You can also substitute chicken thighs.

Heat 3 tablespoons oil in heavy large skillet over medium-high heat. Add onion and garlic and sauté until tender and golden, about 5 minutes. Add chopped rabbit; sauté until light brown, about 4 minutes. Add wine and boil until slightly reduced, about 3 minutes. Stir in chopped tomatoes, crushed tomatoes, 1 cup basil, dried red pepper and remaining 2 tablespoons oil. Bring to boil. Reduce heat to medium-low. Simmer until sauce thickens slightly, stirring occasionally, about 30 minutes. Season sauce generously with salt and pepper.

Meanwhile, cook pasta in large pot of boiling salted water until tender but still firm to bite. Drain. Return pasta to pot. Add sauce; toss to coat. Transfer to bowl. Sprinkle with remaining ½ cup basil and Parmesan cheese.

4 TO 6 SERVINGS

Spaghetti with Tuna, Tomatoes, Capers and Basil

Serve this simple-to-prepare pasta (pictured opposite) with crusty bread, mixed olives and a glass of Italian rosé (called *rosato*) or Pinot Grigio.

2	pounds tomatoes, halved, seeded, very thinly sliced
2	6-ounce cans solid white tuna packed in oil, drained, separated into chunks
½	cup extra-virgin olive oil
4	anchovy fillets, minced
2	small garlic cloves, minced
¼	cup chopped drained capers
1¼	pounds spaghetti
2	cups coarsely chopped fresh basil (from 3 large bunches)

Gently mix first 6 ingredients in large bowl. Season tuna-tomato mixture to taste with salt and pepper. Let stand 1 hour at room temperature.

Cook spaghetti in large pot of boiling salted water until tender but still firm to bite, stirring occasionally. Drain spaghetti; return to same pot. Add tuna-tomato mixture and basil. Toss to combine. Season to taste with salt and pepper. Transfer to bowl and serve.

6 SERVINGS

Linguine with Peperoncini and Bacon

½	pound bacon, coarsely chopped
1	small red onion, chopped
4	large garlic cloves, chopped
8	peperoncini from jar, drained, stemmed, seeded, chopped
2	14.5-ounce cans diced tomatoes in juice
12	ounces freshly cooked linguine
	Grated Parmesan cheese

Sauté bacon in heavy large pot over medium-high heat until crisp and brown. Using slotted spoon, transfer bacon to paper towels to drain. Spoon off all but 3 tablespoons drippings from pot. Add onion and garlic to drippings. Sauté over medium-high heat until onion begins to soften, about 4 minutes. Add peperoncini and stir 1 minute. Add tomatoes with juices and bacon. Simmer sauce 2 minutes to blend flavors. Season sauce with salt and pepper. Reduce heat to medium-low. Add linguine; toss until pasta is coated with sauce. Transfer linguine to bowl; sprinkle with Parmesan cheese. Serve, passing more cheese separately.

4 SERVINGS

Roll Models

Many people consider pizza their favorite food. Yet few folks make it at home—probably because traditional pizza crust is a yeast-leavened dough that takes effort and requires time to mix, knead and let rise.

A handful of products, however, now make it easier to enjoy freshly baked pizza at home. Pre-baked crusts make excellent pizza foundations and stand up well to the baking time and temperature necessary for toppings to turn golden and bubbly. The Italian flatbread known as focaccia is equally good in that role; halved French bread, English muffins and even bagels work as pizza crusts, too. And don't overlook the freezer case, which contains frozen bread or pizza dough that can be defrosted and stretched into the foundation for an excellent homemade pizza. Or make pizza crust dough ahead of time and freeze it. Remove it from the freezer and let it thaw at room temperature about 15 minutes before rolling out or patting into a pan for pre-baking.

Spicy Sausage and Gorgonzola Pizza

3	Italian hot sausages (about 12 ounces), casings removed
1	10-ounce purchased fully baked thin pizza crust
1¼	cups purchased refrigerated marinara sauce
1¼	cups grated mozzarella cheese (about 5 ounces)
½	cup thinly sliced fresh basil leaves
1	cup crumbled Gorgonzola cheese (about 4 ounces)
¼	cup pitted Kalamata olives or other brine-cured black olives, halved
4	thin rounds green bell pepper, halved

Position rack in center of oven and preheat to 425°F. Sauté sausage in large skillet over medium-high heat until just cooked through, breaking into ½-inch pieces with back of spoon, about 10 minutes. Drain off fat; set sausage aside. Place pizza crust on rimless baking sheet. Leaving ¾-inch plain border, spread 1 cup sauce over crust. Top with ¾ cup mozzarella, ¾ of basil, sausage, ½ cup Gorgonzola, olives, ½ cup mozzarella, bell pepper and ½ cup Gorgonzola. Drizzle remaining ¼ cup sauce over. Bake pizza until crust is crisp and topping is heated through, about 13 minutes. Sprinkle with remaining basil and serve.

6 SERVINGS

The Flavors of Bon Appétit 2002

Goat Cheese Pizzas with Indian-spiced Tomatoes and Mustard Greens

The tart flavor of goat cheese complements the cumin and peppers in this imaginative variation on traditional Indian fare.

TOPPING

3	tablespoons vegetable oil
5	large shallots, finely chopped
3½	tablespoons minced fresh ginger
4	garlic cloves, minced
2½	teaspoons ground coriander
2½	teaspoons ground cumin
¼	teaspoon dried crushed red pepper
2½	cups canned crushed tomatoes with added puree
2	cups chopped mustard greens

FLATBREADS

2	cups semolina flour (pasta flour)*
1	cup all purpose flour
1	teaspoon salt
1	teaspoon dry mustard
1¼	cups water, room temperature
3	tablespoons chopped fresh cilantro
8	ounces soft fresh goat cheese (such as Montrachet), crumbled

FOR TOPPING: Heat oil in large skillet over medium-high heat. Add shallots and next 5 ingredients; sauté 3 minutes. Add tomatoes; reduce heat and simmer 5 minutes to thicken. Add greens; stir until wilted, 5 minutes. Season with salt and pepper. (*Can be prepared 1 day ahead. Cover; chill.*)

FOR FLATBREADS: Mix first 4 ingredients in large bowl. Stir in 1¼ cups water and cilantro. Knead in bowl until smooth, about 5 minutes. Cover with kitchen towel; let rest 30 minutes. Divide dough into 4 pieces; roll each into ball. Cover loosely with plastic wrap; let rest on work surface 30 minutes. Roll out each dough ball on lightly floured surface to 9-inch round.

Heat large dry nonstick skillet over medium heat. Add 1 flatbread round to skillet; cook until bottom of bread is golden brown in spots and bread puffs slightly, about 4 minutes. Turn bread over; cook until bottom is brown in spots, about 3 minutes. Repeat with remaining dough.

Preheat oven to 450°F. Place breads on baking sheet. Spread ¼ of topping over each. Sprinkle with cheese. Bake until heated through, about 8 minutes.

Available at specialty foods stores, Italian markets and some supermarkets.

4 SERVINGS

Santa Fe Pizza

1 10-ounce purchased fully baked thin pizza crust
1¾ cups grated sharp cheddar cheese
2 cups roast chicken strips
½ teaspoon ground cumin
½ cup thinly sliced red onion
6 tablespoons frozen corn kernels, thawed, drained
6 tablespoons chopped fresh cilantro
2 large jalapeño chilies, cut into thin rounds, seeded
⅔ cup drained purchased refrigerated fresh salsa

Position rack in center of oven and preheat to 425°F. Place crust on rimless baking sheet. Leaving ¾-inch plain border, sprinkle 1 cup cheese, chicken strips and cumin over crust. Top with onion, 4 tablespoons corn, 4 tablespoons cilantro, ¾ cup cheese, jalapeños and 2 tablespoons corn. Bake pizza until crust is crisp and topping is heated through, about 13 minutes. Top with salsa and remaining 2 tablespoons cilantro.

6 SERVINGS

Goat Cheese and Asparagus Pizza

6 asparagus spears, trimmed, halved lengthwise, cut into 1½-inch pieces
3 tablespoons extra-virgin olive oil
1 10-ounce tube refrigerated pizza crust dough
1 14½-ounce can diced tomatoes with Italian seasonings, drained
1 5.5-ounce log soft fresh goat cheese (such as Montrachet)
3 tablespoons chopped fresh marjoram
¼ teaspoon dried crushed red pepper

Preheat oven to 400°F. Toss asparagus with oil in medium bowl to coat. Unroll pizza dough on baking sheet, forming 9x12-inch rectangle. Spoon tomatoes over dough, leaving ¾-inch plain border. Scatter asparagus over.

Bake pizza 7 minutes. Remove from oven. Crumble goat cheese over pizza. Sprinkle with marjoram and dried red pepper. Bake until crust is golden around edges, about 9 minutes longer.

2 SERVINGS

Pesto Pizza with Crabmeat and Artichoke Hearts

1 10-ounce purchased fully baked thin pizza crust
⅔ cup purchased pesto
8 ounces crabmeat
1 6- to 6½-ounce jar marinated artichoke hearts, drained, sliced
½ cup Kalamata olives or other brine-cured black olives, halved, pitted
⅛ to ¼ teaspoon dried crushed red pepper
1 tablespoon olive oil
1 large red bell pepper, thinly sliced
1½ cups grated mozzarella cheese

Preheat oven to 450°F. Place crust on baking sheet. Spread with pesto, leaving ½-inch plain border. Top evenly with crabmeat, artichokes, olives and dried red pepper. Heat oil in heavy medium skillet over medium-high heat. Add bell pepper and sauté until just tender, about 5 minutes; arrange pepper slices on pizza. Sprinkle cheese over.

Bake pizza until crust is brown and crisp on bottom and topping is heated through, 15 minutes. Transfer pizza to work surface; cut into wedges.

4 TO 6 SERVINGS

Pizza Party for Two

Goat Cheese and Asparagus Pizza
(at left)

Raw Veggies

Chianti

Lemon-Buttermilk Sorbet
(page 179)

Salad of Fall Greens with
Persimmons and Hazelnuts (page 149)

On the Side

Side Dishes

Salads

Breads

Baby Artichokes with Oven-dried Tomatoes and Green-Olive Dressing

Unlike their big brothers, baby artichokes are almost completely edible and require minimal preparation. For this dish, sautéeing the artichokes instead of steaming them adds good flavor.

1 lemon
2 pounds baby artichokes (about 18)
6 tablespoons olive oil
4 garlic cloves, thinly sliced
1 teaspoon dried herbes de Provence*
½ cup canned vegetable broth
⅓ cup dry white wine

8 ounces fresh crimini mushrooms, quartered
Oven-dried Tomatoes (see recipe opposite)
Green-Olive Dressing (see recipe opposite)
Lemon wedges

Fill large bowl with cold water. Cut lemon in half; squeeze juice into water, then add lemon halves. Cut off stem and top quarter from 1 artichoke. Bend back dark green outer leaves and snap off at artichoke base until only pale green and yellow leaves remain. Cut artichoke lengthwise in half. Remove any purple-tipped leaves from center of artichoke. Place artichoke

Side Dishes

halves in lemon water. Repeat with remaining artichokes. Drain artichokes well. Heat 3 tablespoons oil in heavy large pot over medium heat. Add artichokes; sprinkle with salt and pepper and sauté 3 minutes. Add garlic and herbes de Provence; sauté until artichokes begin to brown slightly, about 6 minutes. Add broth and wine; bring to boil. Reduce heat; cover and simmer until artichokes are tender and most liquid is absorbed, about 10 minutes. Uncover and simmer until all liquid is absorbed, about 3 minutes. Transfer artichokes to platter; cover and keep warm.

Heat remaining 3 tablespoons oil in same pot over medium-high heat. Add mushrooms and sauté until tender and golden brown, about 8 minutes; season to taste with salt and pepper. Transfer mushrooms and Oven-dried Tomatoes to platter with artichokes. Spoon Green-Olive Dressing over. Garnish with lemon slices and serve.

A dried herb mixture available at specialty foods stores and in the spice section of some supermarkets. A combination of dried thyme, basil, savory and fennel seeds can be substituted.

4 SERVINGS

Oven-dried Tomatoes

    1 pound plum tomatoes, cut lengthwise in half, seeded
    2 tablespoons olive oil

Preheat oven to 300°F. Lightly oil rimmed baking sheet. Arrange tomatoes, cut side up, on prepared sheet. Drizzle 2 tablespoons oil over tomatoes. Sprinkle with salt and pepper. Bake until tomatoes look slightly shriveled and are slightly brown around edges, about 1 hour 30 minutes. *(Can be prepared 3 days ahead. Cover; chill. Bring to room temperature before using.)*

4 SERVINGS

Green-Olive Dressing

    ²/₃ cup extra-virgin olive oil
    ¼ cup seeded chopped tomato
    ¼ cup finely chopped pitted brine-cured green olives (such as Sicilian)
    2 teaspoons grated lemon peel

Mix all ingredients in small bowl. Season to taste with salt and pepper. Let stand 2 hours at room temperature to blend flavors. *(Can be prepared 3 days ahead. Cover and chill. Bring to room temperature before using.)*

MAKES ABOUT 1 CUP

Dinner in the Loft for Four

Double-Salmon Dip
(page 20)

Bagel Chips

Grilled Chicken or Turkey Sausages

Baby Artichokes with Oven-dried Tomatoes and Green-Olive Dressing
(opposite; pictured opposite)

Pinot Grigio

Fruit Tartlets

Elegant Dinner for Eight

Potato, Celery Root and Fontina Gratin

 2   tablespoons (¼ stick) butter
 2   cups thinly sliced leeks (white and pale green parts only; about 2 large)
 2   pounds russet potatoes, peeled, thinly sliced
1¼   cups whipping cream
1¼   cups canned low-salt chicken broth
 1   14- to 16-ounce celery root, peeled, halved lengthwise, thinly sliced
 1   teaspoon salt
 ½   teaspoon ground black pepper
 ⅛   teaspoon celery seeds
 ⅛   teaspoon grated nutmeg
1½   cups grated Fontina cheese (about 6 ounces)

Preheat oven to 400°F. Lightly butter 11x7x2-inch glass baking dish. Melt butter in heavy large pot over medium-high heat. Add leeks and sauté until wilted, about 4 minutes. Add potatoes and next 7 ingredients; bring to boil, stirring occasionally to separate vegetables. Boil 5 minutes. Transfer half of potato mixture to prepared baking dish. Sprinkle with half of cheese. Top with remaining potato mixture. Cover with foil and place on large baking sheet. Bake 45 minutes. Uncover and bake until juices thicken, about 15 minutes longer. Sprinkle with remaining cheese and bake until golden brown, about 15 minutes longer. Let stand 10 minutes and serve.

6 TO 8 SERVINGS

Sesame Jasmine Rice with Soybeans

 2   cups water
1½   cups jasmine rice or long-grain white rice
 1   pound boiled soybeans (edamame), shelled (about 8 ounces)
 1   tablespoon peanut oil
 ¾   teaspoon salt
1½   tablespoons sesame seeds, toasted

Combine 2 cups water, rice, soybeans, oil and salt in large saucepan. Bring to boil over high heat, stirring occasionally. Reduce heat to medium, cover and simmer until rice is tender, about 15 minutes. Remove from heat. Let stand, covered, 5 minutes. Fluff rice with fork. Stir in sesame seeds; season to taste with salt and pepper.

6 SERVINGS

Sweet Maple Carrots

1½ pounds carrots, peeled, cut into ½-inch-thick rounds
⅓ cup water
3 tablespoons unsalted butter
2 tablespoons pure maple syrup
1 tablespoon dark brown sugar

Bring all ingredients to boil in heavy large skillet. Reduce heat to medium; cover and simmer until carrots are crisp-tender, about 8 minutes. Uncover; cook until juices are reduced to glaze, about 5 minutes. Season carrots to taste with salt and pepper and serve.

6 SERVINGS

Lemon-Sage Green Beans

1½ pounds green beans, trimmed
1 lemon
3 tablespoons butter
1 tablespoon finely sliced fresh sage leaves
    (about 6 large leaves)

Cook green beans in large pot of boiling salted water until crisp-tender, about 5 minutes. Drain. Using vegetable peeler, cut off lemon peel in strips. Slice strips very thinly. Melt butter in large skillet over medium-high heat. Add 1½ tablespoons peel and sage; sauté until fragrant, about 2 minutes. Add beans; toss until heated through. Season with salt and pepper.

6 SERVINGS

Asparagus and Wild Mushroom Fricassee

An assortment of wild mushrooms is essential to the success of this dish (pictured opposite), since much of the flavor rests on the combinations.

1 pound medium asparagus, tough ends trimmed
2 teaspoons olive oil

3 tablespoons butter
1 large shallot, minced
12 ounces assorted wild mushrooms (such as crimini, oyster, chanterelle and stemmed shiitake), sliced
½ cup dry white wine
1 tablespoon minced fresh Italian parsley
1 teaspoon minced fresh tarragon

Preheat oven to 475°F. Arrange asparagus on rimmed baking sheet. Drizzle oil over and turn to coat. Sprinkle generously with salt and pepper. Roast until just tender, about 10 minutes.

Meanwhile, melt butter in large skillet over medium-high heat. Add shallot; sauté 1 minute. Add mushrooms; sauté until beginning to brown, about 5 minutes. Cover; cook until mushrooms are tender, about 3 minutes. Add wine; cook uncovered until wine is absorbed, about 2 minutes. Stir in parsley and tarragon. Season to taste with salt and pepper.

Divide asparagus among 4 plates. Top each serving with mushrooms.

4 SERVINGS

Bistro French Fries with Parsley and Garlic

4 medium russet potatoes (about 1¾ pounds), unpeeled
2 tablespoons canola oil

¼ cup chopped fresh parsley
2 garlic cloves, minced
Coarse salt

Position rack in center of oven and preheat to 425°F. Cut potatoes lengthwise into ⅓-inch-thick slices, then cut lengthwise into ⅓-inch-wide strips. Pat potato strips dry with paper towels. Combine potatoes and oil in large bowl; toss to coat well. Divide potatoes between 2 large baking sheets; spread in single layer. Bake until potatoes are deep golden brown, turning and rearranging potatoes frequently, about 40 minutes.

Transfer potatoes to bowl. Toss with parsley, garlic and coarse salt.

4 SERVINGS

Sweet Illusions

So many North Americans refer to sweet potatoes as "yams" that the two terms are sometimes used interchangeably. In fact, they refer to two families of tuberous vegetables.

True sweet potatoes are similar in size to large baking potatoes, but their ends usually taper to thin points. There are two primary varieties. One has a tan skin, a fairly dry yellow flesh, and a mild, nutty flavor that makes it a suitable substitute for common potatoes. The other has a darker, reddish skin and a very sweet orange-colored flesh that makes it especially popular as an accompaniment to festive holiday roasts, especially turkey.

The latter type of sweet potato is the kind often called a yam in North America. True yams, however, are much larger tubers native to Asia and Africa and also grown throughout Latin America and the Caribbean. They have thick skin and sweet flesh that can range in color from white to orange to purple. In spite of their different origins, yams and orange-fleshed sweet potatoes may be successfully substituted for each other.

Roasted Sweet Potatoes with Honey Glaze

2¼ pounds red-skinned sweet potatoes (or yams), peeled, cut into 1½-inch pieces (about 7 cups)
6 tablespoons (¾ stick) butter
3 tablespoons honey
1 teaspoon fresh lemon juice

Preheat oven to 350°F. Arrange sweet potatoes in 13x9x2-inch glass baking dish. Stir butter, honey and lemon juice in heavy small saucepan over medium heat until butter melts. Pour butter mixture over sweet potatoes in dish; toss to coat. Sprinkle sweet potatoes generously with salt and pepper. Bake sweet potatoes until tender when pierced with skewer, stirring and turning occasionally, about 50 minutes.

4 SERVINGS

Baby Potatoes with Parsley and Lemon Butter

3 pounds mixed baby potatoes (such as white- and red-skinned)
6 tablespoons (¾ stick) butter
6 tablespoons chopped fresh parsley
1 tablespoon grated lemon peel
1 tablespoon fresh lemon juice
1½ teaspoons salt
½ teaspoon ground black pepper

Cook potatoes in large pot of boiling salted water until tender, about 20 minutes. Drain. *(Can be prepared 2 hours ahead. Let stand at room temperature.)* Melt butter in large skillet over medium-high heat. Add potatoes, 4 tablespoons parsley, lemon peel, lemon juice, salt and pepper. Cook until potatoes are heated through and beginning to brown, tossing often, about 5 minutes. Transfer to bowl. Sprinkle with 2 tablespoons parsley and serve.

6 SERVINGS

Grilled Corn with Roasted Garlic Butter

   2 large heads of garlic

   4 tablespoons olive oil

  10 tablespoons (1¼ sticks) butter, room temperature

   6 large ears sweet corn, husks removed

Position rack in center of oven and preheat to 350°F. Cut off and discard top quarter of each garlic head. Place garlic in small baking dish. Drizzle with 2 tablespoons oil. Cover dish with foil and bake until garlic is tender, about 1 hour 10 minutes. Cool garlic slightly. Squeeze garlic out of papery skins, letting garlic fall into small bowl. Mash with fork. Stir in butter. Season to taste with salt and pepper. *(Roasted garlic butter can be prepared 2 days ahead. Cover and keep refrigerated. Bring to room temperature before using.)*

Prepare barbecue (medium heat). Brush corn lightly all over with remaining 2 tablespoons oil. Grill corn until brown in spots, turning occasionally, about 12 minutes. Serve hot, passing roasted garlic butter separately.

6 SERVINGS

Mashed Potatoes with Spinach and Cheese

   4 6-ounce bags fresh baby spinach

   4 pounds white-skinned potatoes, peeled, cut into 2-inch pieces

  ½ cup (1 stick) butter

1¼ cups (or more) warm whole milk

   3 cups grated Gruyère cheese (about 12 ounces)

Bring large pot of salted water to boil. Add spinach and cook 1 minute. Drain well. Squeeze out as much water as possible. Set aside.

Cook potatoes in large pot of boiling salted water until very tender, about 30 minutes. Drain well. Return potatoes to pot and mash until almost smooth. Set pot over low heat. Add butter and stir until melted. Gradually add 1¼ cups milk, mashing until smooth. Add cheese and spinach and stir until cheese melts. Thin with more milk, if desired. Season to taste with salt and pepper. Transfer potatoes to bowl.

6 SERVINGS

Supper in the Kitchen for Six

Braised Meatballs in Red-Wine Gravy
(page 40)

Mashed Potatoes with Spinach and Cheese
(at left)

Steamed Vegetables

Multi-grain Rolls

Zinfandel

Blueberry Crisp with Oatmeal and Almond Topping
(page 184)

Thai Cucumber Salad with Roasted Peanuts

Thai Cucumber Salad with Roasted Peanuts (pictured opposite) is the perfect accompaniment to just about any seafood off the grill. Serve it with white rice, beer and, for dessert, lychees, star fruit and melon sprinkled with fresh lime and toasted sesame seeds.

¼ cup fresh lime juice
1½ tablespoons fish sauce (nam pla)*
1½ tablespoons sugar
1½ tablespoons minced seeded jalapeño chili (about 1 large)
2 garlic cloves, minced
1½ English hothouse cucumbers, halved, seeded, thinly sliced
¾ cup sliced red onion
3 tablespoons chopped fresh mint
3 tablespoons coarsely chopped lightly salted roasted peanuts

Whisk first 5 ingredients in medium bowl. Place cucumbers, onion and mint in large bowl. Add dressing and toss to coat. Season salad to taste with salt and pepper. Sprinkle with peanuts and serve.

*Available at Asian markets and in the Asian foods section of many supermarkets.

6 SERVINGS

Potato, Green Bean and Cherry Tomato Salad

1¼ pounds slender green beans, trimmed
2 pounds small red-skinned new potatoes, quartered
8 tablespoons fresh orange juice
3 tablespoons white wine vinegar

1 1-pint basket cherry or teardrop tomatoes, halved
2 tablespoons chopped fresh Italian parsley
⅓ cup olive oil
6 tablespoons drained capers

Cook beans in pot of boiling salted water until crisp-tender, about 4 minutes. Drain. Transfer to medium bowl. Refresh under cold running water. Drain well. Cook potatoes in pot of boiling salted water until just tender, about 8 minutes. Drain. Transfer to large bowl. Add 2 tablespoons orange juice and 2 tablespoons vinegar; toss to coat. Cool to room temperature, occasionally stirring gently.

Add green beans, tomatoes and parsley to potatoes. Whisk remaining 6 tablespoons orange juice, 1 tablespoon vinegar, oil and capers in small bowl to blend. Season dressing with salt and pepper. Add to salad and toss to combine. (Can be made 2 hours ahead. Let stand at room temperature.)

6 SERVINGS

Salads

Green Salad with Tortilla Strips and Queso Fresco

¼ cup Sherry wine vinegar
1 tablespoon grated lime peel
1 serrano chili, seeded, chopped
1½ teaspoons salt
1 teaspoon Worcestershire sauce
½ teaspoon ground black pepper
½ cup olive oil

Vegetable oil
4 5-inch corn tortillas, halved, cut into ¼-inch-thick strips

1 5-ounce bag mixed baby greens
3 ounces queso fresco* or mild feta cheese, crumbled

Blend first 6 ingredients in processor until chili is finely chopped. With machine running, gradually add olive oil in thin steady stream and blend until smooth. Set vinaigrette aside.

Pour enough vegetable oil into heavy skillet to come ¼ inch up sides of skillet. Heat to 350°F. Working in batches, fry tortilla strips until golden, stirring often, about 3 minutes. Transfer to paper towels. Sprinkle with salt.

Place greens in bowl. Toss with vinaigrette. Divide salad among plates. Sprinkle with queso fresco and tortilla strips.

Available at Latin American markets and some supermarkets.

6 SERVINGS

Salad of Winter Greens, Walnuts, Roasted Beets and Goat Cheese

DRESSING

- 3 tablespoons olive oil
- 2 tablespoons white wine vinegar
- 2 tablespoons orange juice
- 1½ teaspoons grated orange peel

SALAD

- 4 2- to 3-inch-diameter beets, unpeeled, scrubbed, all but 1 inch of tops removed
- 1 tablespoon olive oil
- 1 4.5-ounce bag baby lettuces with frisée
- ½ cup walnut pieces, toasted
- 4 ounces chilled soft fresh goat cheese (such as Montrachet), coarsely crumbled
  Thin strips of orange peel

Serve this bistro-style first course with roasted salmon, green beans and an apple tart.

FOR DRESSING: Whisk all ingredients in small bowl to blend. Season dressing to taste with salt and pepper.

FOR SALAD: Preheat oven to 400°F. Toss beets with oil in 11x7-inch metal baking pan. Roast beets until tender, about 1 hour 10 minutes. Cool beets; peel and cut into ½-inch wedges. (*Dressing and beets can be prepared 1 day ahead. Cover separately; chill. Bring both to room temperature before continuing.*) Mix lettuces, walnuts and dressing in large bowl; toss. Divide among plates. Arrange beets around greens; sprinkle with goat cheese and orange peel.

4 SERVINGS

Kielbasa and Lentil Salad
with Warm Mustard-Fennel Dressing

1   1-pound package dried lentils
3   carrots, peeled, thinly sliced
2   celery stalks, chopped
2   teaspoons salt

⅓   cup malt vinegar or apple cider vinegar
2   tablespoons coarse-grained Dijon mustard
1½ teaspoons sugar
2   tablespoons plus ½ cup olive oil
1   pound fully cooked smoked kielbasa sausage, thinly sliced

3   garlic cloves, peeled, flattened
1   large fennel bulb with fronds, bulb and fronds chopped and reserved
      separately
5   green onions, chopped

2   heads frisée lettuce or 1 large head of curly endive, separated into leaves

Place lentils, carrots and celery in heavy large saucepan. Add enough cold water to cover. Stir in salt and bring to boil. Reduce heat, cover and simmer until lentils are just tender, about 20 minutes. Drain. Transfer lentil mixture to bowl. Let stand at room temperature.

Meanwhile, whisk vinegar, mustard and sugar in small bowl to blend; set aside. Heat 2 tablespoons oil in heavy large skillet over medium-high heat. Add kielbasa and sauté until brown, about 5 minutes. Using slotted spoon, transfer to paper towels. Cover to keep warm.

Pour off any fat from skillet and discard. Add remaining ½ cup oil to same skillet; reduce heat to medium. Add garlic and stir until golden, about 2 minutes. Discard garlic. Add fennel bulb to skillet and sauté until crisp-tender, about 4 minutes. Add green onions and stir 1 minute. Whisk in vinegar mixture and bring to boil. Pour fennel mixture over lentils. Toss to coat. Season with salt and pepper.

Line large shallow bowl with frisée leaves. Spoon in lentil salad. Arrange kielbasa slices atop lentils. Sprinkle with chopped fennel fronds and serve.

6 SERVINGS

This salad is hearty enough to make a main course for three or four. Serve it with French Bread with Kalamata Olives and Thyme (page 155) for a lovely Sunday night supper.

Apple and Poppy Seed Slaw

8   cups shredded green cabbage (about 1 small head)
3   medium carrots, peeled, coarsely grated (about 2½ cups)
3   medium Granny Smith apples, peeled, cored, coarsely grated
4   green onions, thinly sliced
2   tablespoons apple cider vinegar

⅔   cup sour cream
½   cup mayonnaise
¼   cup frozen apple juice concentrate, thawed
2   tablespoons poppy seeds

Mix cabbage, carrots, apples and green onions in large bowl. Add apple cider vinegar and toss to coat.

Whisk sour cream, mayonnaise, apple juice concentrate and poppy seeds in medium bowl to blend. Add to cabbage mixture and toss to blend. Season to taste with salt and pepper. Cover and refrigerate at least 1 hour. (*Can be prepared 1 day ahead. Keep refrigerated. Toss to blend before serving.*)

8 TO 10 SERVINGS

Arugula and Green Bean Salad with Walnut Oil Dressing

- 1 large shallot, chopped
- ¼ cup walnut oil or olive oil
- 1 tablespoon Champagne vinegar or white wine vinegar
- 1 pound slender green beans, trimmed
- 4 ounces arugula (about 8 cups)
- 3 hard-boiled eggs, peeled, coarsely chopped

Whisk first 3 ingredients in small bowl. Season dressing to taste. Cook beans in boiling salted water until crisp-tender, about 6 minutes. Drain. Refresh under cold running water. Drain well. Transfer to bowl. Add arugula and half of eggs. Drizzle with dressing; toss. Top with remaining eggs.

6 SERVINGS

Endive Salad with Orange-Ginger Dressing

- 1½ cups orange juice
- 1 tablespoon sugar
- 1 tablespoon chopped peeled fresh ginger
- ½ teaspoon grated orange peel
- 2 teaspoons fresh lemon juice
- 1 teaspoon Dijon mustard
- ¼ cup fresh lime juice
- 8 cups matchstick-size strips Belgian endive (from 8 large heads)
- 2 cups coarsely grated peeled Granny Smith apples (from about 4 apples)
- 5 tablespoons chopped fresh parsley
- 4 oranges, peeled, sliced into ½-inch-thick rounds
- ¼ cup chopped toasted hazelnuts

Simmer orange juice, sugar, ginger and orange peel in medium saucepan over medium-high heat until liquid is reduced to ³/4 cup, stirring occasionally, about 15 minutes. Whisk in lemon juice and mustard. Boil dressing 2 minutes; cool. (*Can be prepared 2 days ahead; cover and refrigerate.*) Mix ¹/2 cup dressing and lime juice in large bowl (reserve remaining dressing for another use). Add endive, grated apples and 4 tablespoons parsley; toss to combine. Place salad on platter and surround with orange rounds. Sprinkle with hazelnuts and remaining 1 tablespoon parsley.

12 SERVINGS

Potato, Bacon and Chive Salad

2 pounds small (about 2-inch-diameter) white-skinned potatoes

4 bacon slices, chopped
1 medium onion, chopped
½ cup canned beef broth
½ cup white wine vinegar
¾ cup chopped fresh chives

Cook potatoes in large saucepan of boiling salted water until tender, about 30 minutes. Drain. Cool 15 minutes. Peel while still warm, then cut into ⅓-inch-thick slices. Transfer to medium bowl.

Meanwhile, cook bacon in medium skillet over medium-high heat until beginning to brown, about 5 minutes. Add onion; reduce heat to medium-low. Sauté onion until translucent, about 3 minutes. Add broth and vinegar; bring to boil. Pour hot dressing over potatoes; toss gently. Fold in ½ cup chives. Season with salt and pepper. Let stand until broth mixture is absorbed, occasionally tossing gently, about 30 minutes. Sprinkle salad with remaining ¼ cup chives. Toss gently and serve.

4 SERVINGS

Spring Greens
with Soppressata and Grapefruit

2   large red grapefruit

1   small shallot, minced
1   tablespoon white wine vinegar
    Additional fresh grapefruit juice
1   teaspoon minced fresh tarragon
6   tablespoons walnut oil or olive oil

8   cups (packed) mixed baby greens (about 5 ounces)
4   ounces thinly sliced soppressata or other Italian salami, cut into thin strips
    Parmesan cheese shavings

Cut peel and white pith from grapefruit. Holding grapefruit over bowl to catch juices, cut between membranes to release segments.

Combine shallot and vinegar in small bowl. Let stand 15 minutes. Add enough additional grapefruit juice to collected juices to measure $1/4$ cup; whisk into vinegar. Add tarragon. Whisk in oil. Season with salt and pepper.

Place greens in large bowl. Drizzle $2/3$ of dressing over and toss to coat. Divide salad among 4 plates. Scatter soppressata over each. Top with grapefruit and Parmesan. Drizzle remaining dressing over and serve.

4 SERVINGS

Salad Daze

Throughout Provence, market stalls display jumbles of tiny salad greens labeled *mesclun* (pronounced *mehz-clan*), meaning "mixture." The term is deliberately vague: Mesclun may include any of several types of leaves, their different shapes, colors, textures and flavors adding delightful variety to salads.

Outside Provence, many markets today sell their own versions of mesclun, or "baby salad greens." Among the many leaves present (along with occasional sprigs of delicate herbs such as chervil), you may find the following.

- Arugula: Peppery greens resembling little oak leaves.
- Chicory: Long-stemmed, frilly, bitter-tasting leaves.
- Dandelion: Slender, pleasantly tangy notch-edged leaves.
- *Frisée:* Young, pale and fairly mild-tasting.
- *Mâche:* Mild, tender, almost juicy oval leaves, also called lamb's lettuce or corn salad.
- Radicchio: Crisp, bright purple, slightly bitter leaves.
- Spinach: Tender baby specimens of the nutrient-rich, dark green, distinctively flavored leaf.
- Watercress: Sprigs covered with dark green, peppery, refreshingly crisp little leaves.

Best Dressed

A well-made vinaigrette can transform assorted greens and other ingredients into salads of distinction. It's simply composed of vinegar, seasonings and oil (ranging from three to five times the quantity of vinegar used).

Your choices for these three elements, however, will allow you to mix vinaigrettes to suit your taste.

- Vinegar: Start with a good-quality vinegar. Experiment with sweet, complex-tasting balsamic vinegar; rich, woodsy Sherry wine vinegar; sprightly Champagne vinegar; or sharp, clean-tasting Asian rice vinegars. Or try vinegar infused with fruit. Citrus juices—lemon in particular—make excellent substitutes for vinegar.
- Seasonings: Dissolve salt or sugar in the vinegar before mixing in the oil. Dijon mustard adds flavor and creamy body. Stir in chopped fresh or dried herbs; minced or roasted garlic, shallot or onion; minced fresh or crushed dried chilies; roasted peppers; and black or white pepper, as well as your choice of other ground spices.
- Oil: Olive oil is the classic choice; those infused with herbs or garlic have even more flavor. Oils from toasted nuts such as walnuts or hazelnuts add rich, earthy flavor. Or for a milder taste, try a flavorless vegetable oil.

Endive and Scallop Salad with Champagne Vinaigrette

½ cup canola oil
1 plum tomato, chopped
¼ cup Champagne vinegar
1 teaspoon honey

¼ cup Johannisberg Riesling wine
¼ cup olive oil
1 medium shallot, chopped
12 ounces sea scallops, each cut horizontally in half

8 small heads of Belgian endive, trimmed, cored, leaves separated
1 5-ounce bag mixed baby greens (about 10 cups)
3 plum tomatoes, halved, sliced
1 red bell pepper, thinly sliced
½ small red onion, thinly sliced

Puree first 4 ingredients in blender until smooth. (*Can be prepared 2 days ahead. Cover; chill. Bring to room temperature and whisk before using.*)

Bring wine, olive oil and shallot to simmer in large skillet over medium-high heat. Add scallops; simmer until opaque in center, about 1 minute. Using slotted spoon, transfer scallops to medium bowl, reserving juices in

148

skillet; cool scallops and juices. Whisk ⅓ cup juices into vinaigrette. Season with salt and pepper. Toss scallops with 3 tablespoons vinaigrette.

Line each of 8 plates with 5 endive leaves. Combine remaining endive leaves, greens, tomatoes, bell pepper and onion in large bowl. Toss with enough vinaigrette to coat salad. Divide salad among plates. Divide scallops among salads and serve.

8 SERVINGS

Salad of Fall Greens with Persimmons and Hazelnuts

¾ cup fresh tangerine juice

1 tablespoon grated tangerine peel

¾ cup vegetable oil

2 tablespoons hazelnut oil or walnut oil

2 tablespoons balsamic vinegar

½ teaspoon salt

¼ teaspoon ground cinnamon

1 head of escarole (about 11 ounces), torn into 2-inch pieces (about 12 cups)

1 large bunch watercress, stemmed (about 6 cups)

1 5-ounce bag mixed baby greens

2 Fuyu persimmons, peeled, halved, thinly sliced

½ cup hazelnuts, toasted, skin rubbed off

Boil tangerine juice and tangerine peel in heavy small saucepan over medium-high heat until reduced to ¼ cup, about 5 minutes. Transfer to medium bowl. Whisk in next 5 ingredients. Season dressing with pepper. (*Can be prepared 1 day ahead. Cover; chill. Rewhisk before using.*)

Place all greens and half of persimmon slices in large bowl. Add dressing and toss to coat. Divide salad among plates. Top each with remaining persimmon slices and hazelnuts and serve.

10 TO 12 SERVINGS

The persimmons in this salad (pictured on page 128) complement the greens with their tangy sweetness. The dressing can be made a day ahead.

Blood Orange and Blue Cheese Salad

This salad (pictured opposite) is most beautiful when prepared with blood oranges, but if they aren't available, don't abandon the dish. Use any kind of orange in the salad.

10 cups (packed) arugula (about 6 ounces)
½ cup crumbled blue cheese
2 blood oranges
¼ cup olive oil
¼ cup fresh lemon juice

Combine arugula and cheese in large bowl. Remove peel and white pith from oranges. Cut between orange membranes to release segments into bowl with arugula and cheese. Pour oil and lemon juice over salad; toss to blend. Season salad to taste with salt and pepper.

6 SERVINGS

Family-Style Greek Salad

½ cup olive oil
¼ cup red wine vinegar
1 teaspoon garlic powder
1 teaspoon dried oregano

1 large head iceberg lettuce, torn into 1-inch pieces
2 medium cucumbers, peeled, halved, seeded, thinly sliced
4 large tomatoes (1¼ pounds), cut into thin wedges
1 large red onion, sliced paper-thin
12 ounces feta cheese, crumbled
¾ cup large round black Greek olives or other brine-cured black olives
¼ cup fresh lemon juice

Whisk oil, vinegar, garlic powder and oregano in small bowl to blend. Season vinaigrette to taste with salt and pepper.

Combine lettuce, cucumbers, tomatoes, onion, cheese and olives in very large bowl. Drizzle with lemon juice and toss to combine. Add vinaigrette to salad and toss to coat.

12 SERVINGS

Whole Wheat Bread
with Raisins and Walnuts

Spritzing the oven with water creates a more humid environment, which in turn gives this bread a nice crust. Use a spray bottle filled with tap water.

1¼ cups lukewarm water (85°F to 95°F)

1 tablespoon active dry yeast (for do-ahead version) or quick-rising dry yeast (for same-day version)

1 cup warm whole milk (105°F to 115°F)

2 tablespoons honey

1 tablespoon salt

¼ cup (½ stick) unsalted butter, melted, cooled slightly

1½ cups whole wheat flour

½ cup rye flour

½ cup oat bran

1 tablespoon unsweetened cocoa powder

2½ cups (about) bread flour

½ cup raisins

½ cup chopped walnuts

Nonstick vegetable oil spray

Stir 1¼ cups lukewarm water and yeast in large bowl to blend. Stir in warm milk, honey and salt, then melted butter. Add whole wheat flour and stir vigorously with wooden spoon until well incorporated. Add rye flour, oat bran and cocoa powder and stir until well blended. Add enough bread flour, ½ cup at a time, to form moist and sticky dough, stirring vigorously with wooden spoon until well incorporated. Mix in raisins and walnuts. Cover bowl with plastic wrap. *For do-ahead version*: Refrigerate dough overnight. *For same-day version*: Let dough rise in warm draft-free area until doubled in volume, about 1 hour (do not punch down dough).

Spray 9x5x3-inch metal loaf pan with nonstick spray. Transfer dough to prepared pan, being careful not to deflate dough. Cover loaf pan loosely with plastic wrap. Let rise in warm draft-free area until dough is puffed and almost reaches top of pan, about 45 minutes for refrigerated dough or 20 minutes for room-temperature dough.

Meanwhile, position rack in center of oven and preheat to 500°F. Generously spray inside of oven with water (about 8 sprays); immediately place bread in oven. Reduce oven temperature to 400°F and bake bread until top is deep brown and crusty and tester inserted into center comes out clean, about 45 minutes. Cool in pan on rack 10 minutes. Turn bread out onto rack and cool completely.

MAKES 1 LOAF

Cinnamon Streusel Buns

½ cup lukewarm water (85°F to 95°F)
2 teaspoons active dry yeast
1½ cups lukewarm milk (85°F to 95°F)
1¼ cups (2½ sticks) unsalted butter, melted
½ cup sugar
1½ teaspoons salt
2 large eggs
5½ cups (about) all purpose flour

2¼ cups (packed) golden brown sugar
2 cups pecans, toasted, chopped (about 8 ounces)
4½ teaspoons ground cinnamon

Stir ½ cup lukewarm water and yeast in large bowl to blend. Whisk in lukewarm milk, ½ cup melted butter, sugar and salt, then eggs. Add enough flour, ½ cup at a time, to form smooth but very sticky dough, stirring vigorously with wooden spoon. Butter large bowl. Transfer dough to bowl; turn to coat with butter. Cover bowl with plastic wrap. Refrigerate overnight (do not punch down dough).

Mix brown sugar, pecans and cinnamon in 4-cup measuring cup. Stir in remaining ¾ cup melted butter; set aside. Butter 15x10x2-inch glass baking dish. Set aside 2 cups streusel; cover bottom of dish with remaining streusel. Turn dough out onto generously floured surface, scraping bowl with rubber spatula if dough sticks (do not punch down dough). Sprinkle dough lightly with flour. Roll out dough to 14-inch square. Sprinkle reserved 2 cups streusel over dough, leaving ¾-inch plain border on all sides. Roll up jelly-roll style, enclosing streusel completely. Cut rolled dough crosswise in half, then cut each half crosswise into 7 rounds, each about 1 inch thick. Place rounds cut side down and evenly spaced atop streusel in dish (rounds will not cover streusel completely).

Cover dish loosely with plastic wrap. Let dough rise in warm draft-free area until rounds are puffed and almost touching, about 45 minutes.

Meanwhile, position rack in center of oven and preheat to 400°F. Bake buns 10 minutes. Reduce oven temperature to 375°F. Continue to bake buns until golden brown, about 20 minutes longer. Immediately place large baking sheet atop dish with buns. Invert buns onto baking sheet. Cool at least 30 minutes. Serve warm or at room temperature.

MAKES 14

French Bread
with Kalamata Olives and Thyme

1   cup whole milk

2   teaspoons (¼ stick) butter

2   teaspoons sugar

1   cup water, room temperature

2   teaspoons active dry yeast (for do-ahead version) or quick-rising dry yeast (for same-day version)

¾   cup chopped pitted Kalamata olives or other brine-cured black olives

2   teaspoons chopped fresh thyme

2   teaspoons salt

4   cups (or more) all purpose flour
    Olive oil

1   egg white, beaten to blend

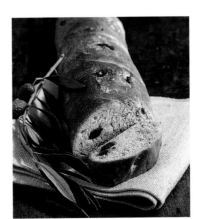

Bring milk to simmer in small saucepan. Add butter and sugar; stir until butter melts. Pour mixture into large bowl. Add 1 cup room-temperature water and cool mixture until lukewarm (85°F to 95°F), about 10 minutes. Add yeast; stir to blend. Stir in olives, thyme and salt. Add 1 cup flour. Using wooden spoon, stir until flour is incorporated. Add 3 cups flour, 1 cup at a time, stirring vigorously with wooden spoon until incorporated after each addition. If necessary, add up to ½ cup more flour until dough is smooth and begins to pull away from sides of bowl. Oil another large bowl. Transfer dough to oiled bowl; turn to coat. Cover bowl tightly with plastic wrap. *For do-ahead version*: Chill dough overnight. *For same-day version*: Let dough rise in warm draft-free area until doubled in volume, about 45 minutes (do not punch down dough).

Position rack in center of oven and preheat to 500°F. Oil large baking sheet. Turn dough out onto floured work surface (to avoid deflating, do not punch down or knead dough). Divide dough into 2 equal pieces. Gently form (do not knead) each piece into baguette 15 inches long by 2¼ to 2½ inches wide (dough will not be smooth). Transfer baguettes to baking sheet, spacing evenly apart. Cover loosely with plastic wrap. Let rise in warm draft-free area until slightly puffed, 30 minutes for chilled dough or 15 minutes for room-temperature dough.

Brush top of each loaf with egg white. Spray inside of oven with water (about 8 sprays); immediately place loaves in oven. Bake 10 minutes. Reduce oven temperature to 400°F; continue to bake until loaves are deep golden and sound hollow when tapped, 35 minutes. Cool on rack.

MAKES 2 SMALL LOAVES

Catchers of the Rye

Gone are the days of all purpose flour or nothing on supermarket shelves. Here's a quick rundown of the wonderful world of flours milled from wheat and other grains.

Wheat Flours

• All Purpose Flour: A white milled blend of soft and hard wheat grains from which the bran and germ have been removed; it delivers consistent results for a wide range of baking needs.

• Bread Flour: An unbleached flour from gluten-rich hard wheat, ideal for baking bread. (Gluten gives bread dough its resiliency.)

• Cake Flour: Soft wheat flour blended with a little cornstarch, tailor-made for light cakes.

• Gluten Flour: Milled from hard wheat treated to diminish its starch content, and high in protein. It is good for people with wheat allergies and may be combined with low-gluten flours.

• Self-rising Flour: A blend of all purpose flour, baking powder and salt; ideal for quickbreads.

• Whole Wheat Flour: Flour milled from wheat grains complete with bran and germ, higher in nutrients but also in particles that

Cracked Pepper Focaccia with Truffle Oil

        2 cups lukewarm water (85°F to 95°F)
        1 tablespoon active dry yeast (for do-ahead version) or quick-rising dry
              yeast (for same-day version)
        4 tablespoons extra-virgin olive oil
        2 tablespoons white or black truffle oil* or olive oil
        1 tablespoon cracked black pepper
        2 teaspoons salt
      4¾ cups (about) bread flour

        1 tablespoon chopped fresh thyme
        2 teaspoons chopped fresh rosemary
        2 teaspoons coarse salt

Stir 2 cups lukewarm water and yeast in large bowl to blend. Mix in 3 tablespoons olive oil, truffle oil, cracked pepper and 2 teaspoons salt. Add 1 cup flour. Using wooden spoon, stir vigorously until well incorporated. Add enough of remaining 3¾ cups flour, ½ cup at a time, stirring vigorously until well incorporated, to form dough that is soft, sticky and not completely smooth. Oil large bowl. Scrape dough into oiled bowl and cover with plastic wrap. *For do-ahead version*: Chill dough overnight. Allow dough to come to room temperature in warm draft-free area before proceeding. *For same-day version*: Let dough rise in warm draft-free area

until doubled in volume, about 45 minutes (do not punch down dough).

Lightly oil 15x10x1-inch baking sheet. Slide out dough onto prepared baking sheet (dough will be soft and will easily slide out onto sheet; do not punch down or knead dough). Gently pull and stretch dough so that it almost covers baking sheet. Press fingertips all over top of dough to form indentations. Brush top of focaccia with remaining 1 tablespoon olive oil. Sprinkle

The Flavors of Bon Appétit 2002

with thyme, rosemary and coarse salt. Cover dough loosely with plastic wrap. Let dough rise in warm draft-free area until puffed, about 30 minutes for refrigerated dough or about 15 minutes for room-temperature dough.

Meanwhile, position rack in center of oven and preheat to 450°F. Bake focaccia until deep golden brown, about 30 minutes. Transfer to rack; cool.

Available at Italian markets, specialty foods stores and some supermarkets.

MAKES 1 LARGE LOAF

Cream Biscuits with Bacon and Roasted Onions

1	pound onions, peeled, cut into ½-inch dice
3	tablespoons chopped fresh parsley
1	tablespoon chopped fresh thyme
1	teaspoon chopped fresh rosemary
2	tablespoons olive oil
6	bacon slices, coarsely chopped
3¾	cups all purpose flour
2	tablespoons baking powder
1	tablespoon sugar
½	teaspoon salt
3	cups chilled whipping cream
1	large egg, beaten to blend (for glaze)

Preheat oven to 350°F. Mix onions, herbs and oil in bowl. Spread on large rimmed baking sheet; sprinkle with salt and pepper. Roast until golden, stirring twice, about 30 minutes. Cool. Maintain oven temperature.

Cook bacon in medium skillet until crisp and brown. Using slotted spoon, transfer bacon to paper towels to drain.

Blend flour, baking powder, sugar and salt in large bowl. Mix in bacon and half of roasted onion mixture. Mix in cream, tossing just until dry ingredients are evenly moistened; do not overmix. Turn dough out onto floured work surface. Knead for 5 turns to combine well. Shape into 18-inch-long log. Cut crosswise into eighteen 1-inch-thick rounds. Arrange rounds on baking sheet, spacing evenly apart. Brush each with glaze; top each with some of remaining onion mixture, pressing to adhere.

Bake biscuits until golden brown, about 20 minutes. Serve biscuits warm or at room temperature.

MAKES 18

interfere with gluten formation, yielding denser, heavier bread; often used in combination with all purpose or bread flour.

Other Flours
(For breads that will rise well, use one part of the following flours to at least four parts wheat flour.)

- Barley Flour: Adds a nutty, malted flavor.
- Buckwheat Flour: Earthy and slightly sour-sweet in flavor.
- Corn Flour: Finer in texture than cornmeal, it adds a golden color and sweet, earthy flavor.
- Oat Flour: Rich, earthy and sweet. It also contributes tender, moist texture.
- Rice Flour: Ground from brown or white rice, it adds sweet, mildly nutlike flavor.
- Rye Flour: A tangy, full-bodied, distinctively sour flour with some gluten, requiring only one part of white wheat flour for every one to two parts of rye.

Miniature Pumpkin Breads

You'll need six baby loaf pans for this recipe. Look for disposable ones at the market.

Nonstick vegetable oil spray

3 cups raw pumpkin seeds (pepitas; about 15 ounces)

3½ cups unbleached all purpose flour
2 teaspoons baking powder
2 teaspoons baking soda
1½ teaspoons salt
1½ teaspoons ground cinnamon
¾ teaspoon ground nutmeg
3 cups canned pure pumpkin (about 24 ounces)
1 cup sugar
1 cup (packed) golden brown sugar
1 cup vegetable oil
4 large eggs
1 teaspoon minced peeled fresh ginger
¾ cup buttermilk

Preheat oven to 350°F. Spray six 5¾x3¼x2-inch baby loaf pans with nonstick spray. Spread seeds out on rimmed baking sheet. Roast until beginning to color, stirring twice, about 20 minutes. Cool seeds. Set aside ½ cup whole seeds for topping. Using on/off turns, coarsely grind remaining seeds in food processor.

Combine flour, baking powder, baking soda, salt, cinnamon and nut-meg in medium bowl; whisk to blend. Mix in ground pumpkin seeds. Using electric mixer, beat pure pumpkin and both sugars in large bowl until blended. Gradually beat in oil, then eggs 1 at a time, then minced ginger. Stir in dry ingredients in 4 additions alternately with buttermilk in 3 additions. Divide batter among prepared pans. Sprinkle with reserved 1/2 cup whole pumpkin seeds.

Bake breads until tester inserted into center comes out clean, about 1 hour. Cool in pans. (*Can be made 1 day ahead. Cover; store at room temperature.*)

MAKES 6

Chive-Corn Muffins

Nonstick vegetable oil spray
1 cup all purpose flour
1 cup yellow cornmeal
1 tablespoon sugar
2 teaspoons baking powder
1 teaspoon salt
1/2 teaspoon baking soda
1/2 teaspoon cayenne pepper
1/4 cup chopped fresh chives
1 1/2 cups plain yogurt
2 large eggs
3 tablespoons unsalted butter, melted

Cayenne pepper in the batter gives these muffins a nice little kick.

Position rack in center of oven and preheat to 425°F. Spray 10 standard muffin cups (each about 1/3-cup capacity) or 30 mini-muffin cups with nonstick spray. Whisk flour and next 6 ingredients in medium bowl. Stir in chives. In another medium bowl whisk yogurt, eggs and melted butter. Add yogurt mixture to dry ingredients and stir just until blended. Divide batter among prepared muffin cups, using about 1/3 cup batter for each standard muffin cup or about 1 generous tablespoon for each mini-muffin cup.

Bake until muffins are puffed and golden and tester inserted into center comes out clean, about 20 minutes for standard muffins or 14 minutes for mini-muffins. Transfer pans to rack and let muffins cool in pans. (*Muffins can be prepared 4 hours ahead. Leave muffins in pans; let stand at room temperature. Rewarm in 350°F oven just until warm, about 5 minutes.*) Remove muffins from pans and serve.

MAKES ABOUT 10 STANDARD MUFFINS OR 30 MINI-MUFFINS

Tropical Lime Torte with
Mango Compote (page 189)

Desserts

Pies & Tarts

Fruit Desserts

Cakes

Mousses & Puddings

Frozen Desserts

Cookies

Apple and Prune Tart
with Vanilla Ice Cream and Cognac

1¼ cups all purpose flour
½ teaspoon plus 3 tablespoons sugar
½ teaspoon salt
¼ cup solid vegetable shortening, frozen, cut into ½-inch cubes
¼ cup (½ stick) chilled unsalted butter, cut into ½-inch cubes
3 tablespoons (or more) ice water

12 medium pitted prunes
⅓ cup Cognac or brandy

4 6- to 7-ounce Golden Delicious apples, peeled, quartered, cored, each quarter cut into 3 wedges
3 tablespoons unsalted butter, melted
¼ cup apricot preserves, heated, strained
Vanilla ice cream

Blend flour, ½ teaspoon sugar and salt in processor. Add shortening and chilled butter and blend, using on/off turns, until mixture resembles coarse meal. Add 3 tablespoons ice water. Using on/off turns, blend until moist clumps form, adding more water by ½ tablespoonfuls if dry. Gather dough into ball; flatten into disk. Wrap in plastic and chill 1 hour. (*Can be prepared 1 day ahead. Keep chilled. Let dough soften slightly at room temperature before rolling out.*)

Combine prunes and Cognac in small bowl. Cover; let stand 2 hours, stirring often. Drain prunes, reserving Cognac. Cut prunes in half; set aside. Roll out dough on lightly floured surface to 12-inch round. Transfer to 9-inch-diameter tart pan with removable bottom. Fold in overhang and press, forming double-thick sides; refrigerate 30 minutes.

Preheat oven to 400°F. Mix apples, 3 tablespoons sugar and 2 tablespoons melted butter in large bowl. Arrange apple wedges, overlapping slightly, in concentric circles in crust. Bake tart until apples are just tender, about 1 hour. Tuck prunes into spaces between apples. Brush fruit with 1 tablespoon melted butter. Bake until apples are very tender and crust is golden, about 20 minutes. Transfer tart to rack and cool 15 minutes. Blend 1 tablespoon reserved Cognac into strained preserves for glaze. Brush glaze over warm tart. Serve tart wedges warm or at room temperature with ice cream, drizzling some of reserved Cognac over ice cream.

6 SERVINGS

Pies & Tarts

Pecan-Fig Pie with Brandied Whipped Cream

FILLING

- ¾ cup finely chopped stemmed dried Calimyrna figs (about 5 ounces)
- 2 tablespoons brandy
- 2 tablespoons water
- 1 cup (packed) golden brown sugar
- 1 cup light corn syrup
- 3 large eggs
- ¼ cup (½ stick) unsalted butter, melted, cooled
- 1½ teaspoons vanilla extract
- ¼ teaspoon salt
- 2 cups pecan halves, toasted

- 1 refrigerated pie crust (half of 15-ounce package)

CREAM

- 1 cup chilled whipping cream
- 2 tablespoons sugar
- 1 tablespoon brandy

FOR FILLING: Stir figs, brandy and 2 tablespoons water in small saucepan over low heat until liquid is absorbed, 5 minutes; cool. Mix brown sugar, corn syrup and next 4 ingredients in medium bowl. Stir in pecans, then fig mixture.

Preheat oven to 375°F. Roll out dough on lightly floured surface to 13-inch round. Transfer to 9-inch-diameter deep-dish glass pie dish. Fold edge of dough over, forming double edge, and crimp decoratively, pressing to top edge of dish. Pierce all over with fork. Freeze crust 15 minutes.

Line crust with foil; fill with dried beans or pie weights. Bake until sides are set, about 12 minutes. Remove foil and beans. Bake until crust is pale golden, pressing with back of fork if crust bubbles, about 10 minutes. Reduce oven temperature to 325°F.

Spoon filling into warm crust. Bake until filling is puffed at edges and set in center, about 40 minutes. Let stand until cool, at least 1 hour. (*Can be made 1 day ahead. Cover; chill.*)

FOR CREAM: Beat cream, sugar and brandy in medium bowl. Whisk until peaks form. (*Can be made 4 hours ahead. Cover; chill.*) Serve pie with cream.

8 SERVINGS

A Crush on Cardamom

One of mankind's most ancient and widespread spices, cardamom first traveled in ancient times from its home in India to the Middle East and across the Mediterranean to Greece and Rome. Viking travelers carried it north to Scandinavia more than a millennium ago, and later explorers and traders spread its use to the New World.

As a result, the aromatic, sweet yet slightly musky spice has found its way into a wide variety of dishes throughout the world, from the curries of both the East and West Indies to the traditional coffee of the Arab world, to the meatballs and baked goods of Swedish and German cooks, to the savory rice dishes of North Africa. Even the Indian spiced tea known as *chai*, popular today in an Americanized *latte* form, owes much of its enticing flavor to cardamom.

For reliable flavor, buy the spice in whole seed form or, better still, in seed-packed pods that are easily split to remove the seeds. Grind or crush the seeds as needed to release their warm, heady flavor.

Blood Orange Tart
with Cardamom Pastry Cream

CRUST

1½ cups all purpose flour
2 tablespoons sugar
⅛ teaspoon salt
10 tablespoons (1¼ sticks) chilled unsalted butter, cut into ½-inch cubes
2 tablespoons (or more) ice water
1 large egg yolk

PASTRY CREAM

2 cups whole milk
1 tablespoon cardamom pods, crushed slightly
5 large egg yolks
½ cup sugar
6 tablespoons all purpose flour
2 tablespoons (¼ stick) unsalted butter
1 teaspoon vanilla extract

TOPPING

6 blood oranges or small navel oranges
½ cup apricot preserves, melted, strained
2 teaspoons grenadine (optional)

FOR CRUST: Combine flour, sugar and salt in processor. Add butter and cut in using on/off turns until mixture resembles coarse meal. Whisk 2 tablespoons ice water and egg yolk in small bowl. Add to dry ingredients and blend just until moist clumps form, adding more water by teaspoonfuls if dough is dry. Gather dough into ball; flatten into disk. Wrap in plastic and refrigerate at least 1 hour and up to 1 day.

Preheat oven to 375°F. Roll out dough on lightly floured surface to 13- to 14-inch round. Transfer dough to 11-inch-diameter tart pan with removable bottom. Press in overhang, forming double-thick sides. Pierce dough all over with fork. Freeze crust 30 minutes. Bake until golden brown, pressing with back of fork if crust bubbles or slips, about 30 minutes. Transfer to rack and cool.

FOR PASTRY CREAM: Bring milk and cardamom to boil in medium saucepan over medium-high heat. Remove from heat. Cover and let steep 15 minutes. Strain milk into bowl. Whisk egg yolks, sugar and flour in medium bowl to blend. Gradually whisk in milk. Return to saucepan and cook over medium heat until pastry cream thickens and boils, whisking con-

The Flavors of Bon Appétit 2002

stantly, about 5 minutes. Whisk in butter, then vanilla. Transfer to bowl. Press plastic onto surface. Chill until cold, at least 4 hours and up to 1 day.

FOR TOPPING: Cut peel and white pith from oranges. Slice into ¼-inch-thick rounds. Drain rounds on paper towels. Whisk preserves and grenadine, if desired, in small bowl to blend. Spread pastry cream evenly in tart crust. Arrange oranges in overlapping concentric circles on pastry cream. Brush apricot glaze over oranges. Chill until set, about 15 minutes. (*Can be prepared 6 hours ahead; keep refrigerated.*)

10 SERVINGS

Banana Cream Pie
with Chocolate-Chip-Cookie Crust

Nonstick vegetable oil spray
1 pound purchased frozen semisweet chocolate chip cookie dough, thawed
½ cup chopped walnuts

⅓ cup sugar
¼ cup cornstarch
⅛ teaspoon salt
5 large egg yolks
2⅓ cups whole milk
2 tablespoons (¼ stick) unsalted butter
1 tablespoon dark rum
2 teaspoons vanilla extract

3 medium bananas, peeled, cut into ½-inch-thick slices
1 cup chilled whipping cream
2 tablespoons powdered sugar
Chocolate curls (optional)

Spray 9-inch-diameter glass pie dish with nonstick spray. Arrange ¾ of cookie dough in prepared dish (reserve remaining dough for another use). Press dough evenly onto bottom and up sides of dish, building high-standing dough edge on rim of dish. Sprinkle with nuts; press nuts into dough. Pierce dough all over with toothpick. Freeze crust 1 hour.

Position rack in bottom third of oven and preheat to 350°F. Fold 36-inch-long piece of foil lengthwise into thirds, forming 36x4-inch strip. Place pie dish on baking sheet. Stand foil strip snugly around dish, protecting outer edge of crust; secure overlap with paper clip. Bake crust until golden and dry to touch, about 25 minutes. Cool completely.

Meanwhile, whisk ⅓ cup sugar, cornstarch and salt to blend in heavy medium saucepan. Whisk in egg yolks; gradually add milk, whisking until smooth. Whisk over medium-high heat until custard thickens and boils, about 6 minutes. Remove from heat. Whisk in butter, rum and 1 teaspoon vanilla. Transfer to large bowl; cool custard to lukewarm, whisking occasionally, about 45 minutes.

Spread 1 cup custard in crust. Top with bananas, then remaining custard, covering bananas completely. Chill pie until filling sets, about 2 hours. Beat cream, powdered sugar and remaining 1 teaspoon vanilla in medium bowl to peaks. Spread cream over pie. Chill at least 1 hour and up to 8 hours. Garnish pie with chocolate curls, if desired. Cut into wedges and serve.

8 SERVINGS

Dessert Buffet for a Crowd

Banana Cream Pie with Chocolate-Chip-Cookie Crust
(at left; pictured opposite)

Old-fashioned Coconut Cake
(page 196)

Cinnamon-Chocolate Brownies with Chocolate Ganache
(page 216)

Mango Cheesecake
(page 192)

Platter of Fresh Fruit

Platter of Cookies

Champagne and Coffee

CRUST

1½ cups all purpose flour

2 tablespoons sugar

⅛ teaspoon salt

10 tablespoons (1¼ sticks) chilled unsalted butter, cut into ½-inch cubes

2 tablespoons (or more) ice water

1 large egg yolk

¼ cup guava jelly or crab apple jelly

FILLING

2 8-ounce packages cream cheese, room temperature

⅔ cup sugar

1 large egg

¼ teaspoon vanilla extract

½ cup sour cream

TOPPING

¼ cup guava jelly or crab apple jelly

3 small red-fleshed papayas, halved, peeled, seeded, cut lengthwise into ¼-inch-thick slices

2 kiwis, peeled, cut into ¼-inch-thick rounds

1 large ripe mango, halved, pitted, peeled, diced

2 passion fruits, halved (optional)

FOR CRUST: Combine flour, sugar and salt in processor. Add butter and cut in using on/off turns until mixture resembles coarse meal. Whisk 2 tablespoons ice water and egg yolk in small bowl. Add yolk mixture to dry ingredients and blend just until soft moist clumps form, adding more water by teaspoonfuls if dough is dry. Gather dough into ball; flatten into disk. Wrap in plastic and refrigerate 1 hour.

Preheat oven to 375°F. Roll out dough on lightly floured surface to 13- to 14-inch round. Transfer dough to 11-inch-diameter tart pan with removable bottom. Press in overhang, forming double-thick sides. Pierce crust all over with fork. Freeze 30 minutes. Bake crust until golden, pressing with back of fork if crust bubbles or slips, 30 minutes. Transfer to rack. Spread jelly over bottom of crust and cool. Reduce oven temperature to 350°F.

FOR FILLING: Using electric mixer, beat cream cheese in large bowl until smooth. Add sugar and beat until light and fluffy. Beat in egg, then vanilla. Add sour cream and beat just to blend.

Pour filling into tart crust. Bake until filling is slightly puffed and center moves slightly when pan is shaken gently, about 35 minutes. Transfer to rack and cool completely. Refrigerate until cold, at least 4 hours. (*Can be prepared 1 day ahead. Cover and keep refrigerated.*)

FOR TOPPING: Melt jelly in heavy small saucepan over low heat. Brush over top of cheesecake. Overlap papaya slices in circle atop tart. Overlap kiwi rounds in center. Sprinkle mango around edge. Spoon pulp of passion fruits into center, if desired. Serve immediately or chill up to 3 hours.

8 TO 10 SERVINGS

Rustic Plum Tart

1¼ cups plus 1 tablespoon all purpose flour
8 tablespoons sugar
¼ teaspoon salt
½ cup (1 stick) chilled unsalted butter, cut into ½-inch cubes
3 tablespoons (about) ice water
1½ pounds plums, halved, pitted, each half cut into 6 slices
½ teaspoon ground ginger
¼ teaspoon ground cinnamon
2 tablespoons (¼ stick) unsalted butter, melted
1 egg, beaten to blend (for glaze)
¼ cup apricot preserves

Blend 1¼ cups flour, 2 tablespoons sugar and salt in processor. Add chilled butter and cut in, using on/off turns, until mixture resembles coarse meal. Add 2 tablespoons water; blend until moist clumps form, adding more water by teaspoonfuls if dry. Gather dough into disk. Wrap in plastic; chill 1 hour.

Preheat oven to 400°F. Toss plums, 4 tablespoons sugar, ginger and cinnamon in bowl. Roll out dough on floured surface to 12½-inch round. Transfer to baking sheet. Mix 1 tablespoon sugar and remaining 1 tablespoon flour in bowl; sprinkle over dough, leaving 2-inch border. Arrange plums in circles on dough, leaving 2-inch border; drizzle with melted butter. Fold dough border in toward center. Brush border with egg glaze; sprinkle with 1 tablespoon sugar. Bake tart until plums are tender and crust is golden, 45 minutes.

Stir preserves in pan over low heat to melt. Brush over plums. Cool tart 1 hour. Run long thin knife under tart to loosen. Transfer tart to plate; serve at room temperature.

6 SERVINGS

This irresistible pie features a delicious homemade marsh-mallow topping and a luscious chocolate filling. Add chocolate shavings for a finishing touch.

CRUST

1½ cups all purpose flour

 5 tablespoons chilled unsalted butter, cut into ½-inch cubes

¼ cup chilled solid vegetable shortening, cut into ½-inch cubes

 1 tablespoon sugar

¼ teaspoon salt

 3 tablespoons (or more) ice water

FILLING

½ cup sugar

¼ cup cornstarch

 1 tablespoon unsweetened cocoa powder

⅛ teaspoon salt

 4 large egg yolks

 2 cups whole milk

½ cup whipping cream

 5 ounces bittersweet (not unsweetened) or semisweet chocolate, chopped

 1 tablespoon unsalted butter

 1 teaspoon vanilla extract

MARSHMALLOW TOPPING

 1 tablespoon plus ⅓ cup water

½ teaspoon unflavored gelatin

 1 cup sugar

⅓ cup light corn syrup

 4 large egg whites (about ½ cup)

 1 teaspoon vanilla extract

 Chocolate shavings (optional)

FOR CRUST: Combine first 5 ingredients in processor. Using on/off turns, blend until mixture resembles coarse meal. Add 3 tablespoons ice water and blend until moist clumps form, adding more water by teaspoonfuls if dough is dry. Gather dough into ball. Flatten into disk. Wrap disk in plastic and refrigerate at least 1 hour and up to 1 day.

Preheat oven to 375°F. Roll out dough on lightly floured surface to 13- to 14-inch round. Transfer dough to 9-inch-diameter deep-dish glass pie dish. Fold dough edge over and crimp decoratively, securing dough edge to rim of dish. Pierce crust all over with fork. Freeze crust 15 minutes. Bake until golden brown, pressing with back of fork if crust bubbles or slips, about 30 minutes. Transfer crust to rack and cool.

FOR FILLING: Whisk sugar, cornstarch, cocoa and salt in heavy medium saucepan to blend. Add egg yolks, milk and cream; whisk until smooth. Whisk over medium heat until mixture thickens and boils, about 6 minutes. Remove from heat. Add chocolate, butter and vanilla; whisk until melted and smooth. Pour filling into crust. Cool on rack.

FOR MARSHMALLOW TOPPING: Place 1 tablespoon water in metal cup; sprinkle gelatin over. Place cup in small skillet; add enough water to skillet to reach depth of ¹/₂ inch. Whisk sugar, corn syrup and ¹/₃ cup water in heavy medium saucepan to blend. Bring to boil over medium heat, stirring until sugar dissolves. Attach candy thermometer to side of pan. Boil without stirring until candy thermometer registers 240°F. While continuing to boil syrup, beat egg whites in large bowl with electric mixer until stiff peaks form. When thermometer in syrup registers 248°F, gradually beat hot syrup into egg whites. Continue to beat until whites are stiff and glossy, about 4 minutes. Beat in vanilla.

Bring water in skillet to simmer. Stir gelatin mixture in cup until gelatin dissolves. Gradually pour gelatin over egg whites and beat until topping is cool, about 8 minutes. Using rubber spatula, gently spread topping over filling, making decorative peaks. Preheat broiler. Broil pie just until topping is light brown, about 1 minute. Chill pie 1 hour. Garnish with chocolate shavings, if desired. (*Can be prepared 1 day ahead. Keep refrigerated. Let stand 1 hour at room temperature before serving.*)

8 SERVINGS

This is an elegant tart with a cookie-like crust. Make the curd and dough a day or two in advance and complete with beautiful strawberries glazed with jam.

CURD

2	large eggs
½	cup sugar
3	tablespoons fresh lemon juice
¼	cup (½ stick) unsalted butter
1½	teaspoons grated lemon peel

CRUST

1½	cups all purpose flour
3	tablespoons sugar
¼	teaspoon salt
½	cup (1 stick) chilled unsalted butter, cut into ½-inch cubes
2	tablespoons (or more) chilled whipping cream
1	large egg yolk

1½	quarts fresh strawberries, stem end of each cut flat
½	cup strawberry jam

FOR CURD: Whisk eggs, sugar and lemon juice in heavy small saucepan to blend. Add butter and lemon peel. Stir over medium heat until curd thickens to pudding consistency, about 8 minutes. Transfer to small bowl. Press plastic wrap onto surface of curd and chill at least 2 hours.

FOR CRUST: Combine flour, sugar and salt in processor; blend 5 seconds. Add butter; using on/off turns, blend until mixture resembles coarse meal. Add 2 tablespoons cream and egg yolk. Blend until moist clumps form, adding more cream by teaspoonfuls if dough is dry. Gather dough into ball; flatten into disk. Wrap in plastic and refrigerate 1 hour. *(Curd and dough can be prepared 2 days ahead. Keep chilled.)*

Roll out dough on lightly floured surface to 13-inch round. Transfer dough to 9-inch-diameter tart pan with removable bottom. Trim overhang to ½ inch. Fold overhang in and press firmly, forming double-thick sides. Pierce crust all over with fork; refrigerate 1 hour.

Preheat oven to 400°F. Bake crust until golden, pressing with back of fork if crust bubbles, about 20 minutes. Cool crust completely on rack.

Spread curd in crust. Stand berries in curd. Strain jam into saucepan; warm briefly to thin. Brush jam over berries. Chill tart until glaze sets, at least 1 hour and up to 6 hours. Release tart from pan and serve.

10 SERVINGS

CRUST

8 whole graham crackers, coarsely broken

¼ cup (packed) golden brown sugar

¼ cup (½ stick) unsalted butter, melted

FILLING AND TOPPING

6 ounces cream cheese, room temperature

⅓ cup sugar

½ cup sour cream

2 teaspoons fresh lemon juice

½ teaspoon vanilla extract

2 ½-pint baskets fresh raspberries

¼ cup seedless raspberry jam

FOR CRUST: Preheat oven to 375°F. Grind crackers and sugar in processor until coarse crumbs form. Add butter and process until crumbs are evenly moistened. Press crumb mixture firmly onto bottom and up sides of 9-inch-diameter tart pan with removable bottom. Bake until crust is firm to touch, about 8 minutes. Cool crust on rack.

FOR FILLING AND TOPPING: Using electric mixer, beat cream cheese and sugar in medium bowl until smooth. Beat in sour cream, lemon juice and vanilla. Spread filling in cooled crust. Chill until firm, at least 4 hours. (*Can be prepared 1 day ahead. Cover; keep chilled.*)

Arrange berries over filling. Whisk jam in small bowl to loose consistency. Drizzle over berries. Serve immediately or chill up to 3 hours.

8 SERVINGS

Peaches-and-Cream Streusel Pie

CRUST

1¼ cups all purpose flour

¼ teaspoon salt

¼ cup (½ stick) chilled unsalted butter, cut into ½-inch cubes

¼ cup solid vegetable shortening, frozen, cut into ½-inch cubes

2 tablespoons (or more) ice water

TOPPING

½ cup sugar

½ cup chopped pecans

⅓ cup all purpose flour

¼ cup old-fashioned oats

¼ cup (½ stick) unsalted butter, melted

FILLING

½ cup sugar

3 tablespoons whipping cream

3 pounds medium peaches

FOR CRUST: Blend flour and salt in processor 5 seconds. Add butter and shortening. Using on/off turns, blend until butter is reduced to pea-size pieces. Add 2 tablespoons ice water; blend until moist clumps form, adding more water by teaspoonfuls if dough is dry. Gather dough into ball; flatten into disk. Wrap in plastic; chill at least 2 hours and up to 1 day.

FOR TOPPING: Stir all ingredients in medium bowl until small clumps form.

FOR FILLING: Combine sugar and cream in large nonstick skillet. Bring medium saucepan of water to boil. Drop 3 peaches into water; blanch 1 minute. Transfer peaches to bowl of ice water. Peel peaches and slice thinly, letting slices drop into sugar-cream mixture. Repeat with remaining peaches. Cook peach filling over medium-high heat until peaches are tender and mixture is reduced almost to glaze, stirring often, 10 minutes. Set aside.

Preheat oven to 375°F. Roll out dough to 14-inch round. Transfer to 9-inch-diameter glass pie dish. Trim overhang to ¾ inch; fold under and crimp. Pierce crust with fork; freeze 10 minutes. Line with foil and beans or pie weights; bake 10 minutes. Remove foil and beans and bake crust until pale golden, pressing with back of fork if crust bubbles, about 10 minutes longer. Spoon peach filling into warm crust. Sprinkle with topping. Place pie on baking sheet and bake until filling is bubbling and topping is golden brown, about 50 minutes. Cool on rack at least 30 minutes.

8 SERVINGS

Rhubarb-Raspberry Jalousie

2 tablespoons (¼ stick) unsalted butter

4 cups ½-inch-thick slices fresh rhubarb (from about 2 pounds)

1 cup raspberry preserves with seeds

¼ cup plus 2 tablespoons sugar

1 sheet frozen puff pastry (half of 17.3-ounce package), thawed

1 large egg, beaten to blend (for glaze)

Vanilla ice cream

Fruit Desserts

Melt butter in heavy medium saucepan over medium heat. Add rhubarb. Cover and simmer until rhubarb is tender and falling apart, about 10 minutes. Add preserves and ¼ cup sugar. Cook uncovered until very thick and reduced to 2 cups, stirring frequently, about 35 minutes. Refrigerate filling uncovered until cold, at least 1 hour. (*Filling can be prepared 2 days ahead. Cover and keep refrigerated.*)

Preheat oven to 400°F. Line large baking sheet with parchment paper. Roll out pastry on lightly floured surface to 16x12-inch rectangle. Cut pastry in half lengthwise, forming two 16x6-inch rectangles. Place 1 rectangle on prepared baking sheet. Leaving 1-inch plain border, spoon filling onto pastry. Brush border with glaze. Top with second rectangle; press edges firmly to seal. Brush edges with glaze. Fold edges over, forming ¹/₂-inch border. Press border with tines of fork to seal. Brush top of pastry with glaze; sprinkle with 2 tablespoons sugar. Using sharp knife, cut 1¹/₂-inch crosswise slits down center of pastry at 2-inch intervals, exposing filling.

Bake pastry until golden brown, about 25 minutes. Cool on sheet to luke-warm, about 45 minutes. Cut crosswise into 6 pieces. Serve with ice cream.

6 SERVINGS

Banana Fritters with Honey and Ice Cream

1 cup warm water (105°F to 115°F)
1 large egg
2 tablespoons vegetable oil
1 teaspoon dry yeast
1 cup all purpose flour
¹/₂ cup sweetened shredded coconut
1 tablespoon sesame seeds
¹/₄ teaspoon ground nutmeg
4 large bananas

  Additional vegetable oil (for frying)
  Honey
  Vanilla ice cream

Whisk 1 cup warm water, egg and 2 tablespoons oil in large bowl to blend. Add yeast, then flour, whisking until smooth. Cover and let stand at room temperature until batter has almost doubled in volume, about 2 hours. Stir in coconut, sesame seeds and nutmeg. Cut bananas on deep diagonal into eighteen ¹/₂-inch-thick slices. (Reserve any remaining bananas for another use.) Add banana slices to batter; stir gently to coat. (*Bananas can be prepared 1 day ahead. Cover and chill.*)

Pour additional vegetable oil into heavy medium saucepan to depth of 1¹/₂ inches. Attach deep-fry thermometer and heat oil to 350°F. Insert fork into 1 banana slice and transfer to oil. Repeat with 5 banana slices. Fry until crisp and golden on all sides, about 3 minutes. Using slotted spoon, transfer fritters to paper-towel-lined plate to drain. Repeat with remaining bananas in 2 more batches. Divide fritters among 6 plates. Drizzle with honey and serve warm with ice cream.

6 SERVINGS

Pacific-Rim Dinner for Eight

Chinese Dumplings or Spring Rolls

Seared Sesame Tofu with Asian Salad
(page 113; triple recipe)

Jasmine Rice

Japanese Beer

Banana Fritters with Honey and Ice Cream
(at left)

Balsamic Strawberries
with Whipped Mascarpone Cheese

Vinegar and berries may seem like an unusual combination, but the mellow balsamic, sweet strawberries and rich mascarpone come together beautifully in this dish—which can be partly prepared two days ahead.

⅓ cup balsamic vinegar

2 teaspoons plus 4 tablespoons sugar

½ teaspoon fresh lemon juice

½ cup chilled mascarpone cheese*

½ cup chilled whipping cream

½ teaspoon vanilla extract

3 1-pint baskets (about 24 ounces) strawberries, hulled, halved

Combine vinegar, 2 teaspoons sugar and lemon juice in heavy small saucepan. Stir over medium heat until sugar dissolves. Boil until syrup is reduced to scant ¼ cup, about 3 minutes. Transfer to small bowl; cool completely. (Can be prepared 2 days ahead. Cover and refrigerate.)

Combine mascarpone, cream, vanilla and 2 tablespoons sugar in medium bowl. Whisk until thick soft peaks form. Cover and refrigerate up to 4 hours.

Combine berries and remaining 2 tablespoons sugar in large bowl; drizzle with balsamic syrup and toss to blend. Let berries stand 30 minutes, stirring occasionally. Divide berries and syrup among 6 goblets. Top with mascarpone mixture and serve.

*Italian cream cheese, available at Italian markets and many supermarkets.

6 SERVINGS

Apricot-Cherry Crisp
with Lemon-Buttermilk Sorbet

16 small ripe apricots (about 3 pounds), halved, pitted
1½ pounds cherries, pitted
⅔ cup sugar
1 tablespoon cornstarch
½ teaspoon ground cardamom
4 cups purchased granola
½ cup (1 stick) unsalted butter, cut into ½-inch cubes
   Lemon-Buttermilk Sorbet (see recipe below)

Preheat oven to 375°F. Place first 5 ingredients in 13x9x2-inch glass baking dish; toss. Blend granola and butter in processor until moist crumbs form. Sprinkle topping evenly over apricot-cherry mixture. Bake until filling bubbles thickly around edges, about 50 minutes. Serve warm or at room temperature with Lemon-Buttermilk Sorbet.

8 SERVINGS

Lemon-Buttermilk Sorbet

2 cups sugar
½ cup fresh lemon juice
2 tablespoons grated lemon peel
4 cups buttermilk

Stir sugar, lemon juice and peel in medium bowl. Add buttermilk; stir until sugar dissolves. Chill until cold, about 4 hours. Process mixture in ice cream maker according to manufacturer's instructions. Transfer to container with lid; freeze. (*Can be prepared 3 days ahead. Keep frozen.*)

MAKES ABOUT 7 CUPS

Whisked Away

Making meringue couldn't be simpler: Beat egg whites until they begin to froth up. Gradually beat in sugar, and then continue beating until the whites form fluffy clouds that hold their shape. Yet with just a little variation on those basics, a wide variety of meringues may emerge.

- Cocoa Meringue: As the meringue reaches the desired consistency, beat in a little unsweetened cocoa powder along with the sugar to make a brown-hued, chocolate-flavored meringue.

- Dacquoise: Beat finely chopped hazelnuts, almonds or other nuts into the meringue to produce a rich-tasting meringue, also known as *japonaise* meringue, that bakes to a light, cookielike texture. It is often layered with buttercream filling to make the pastry with the same name.

- Italian Meringue: Replace granulated or powdered sugar with a sugar syrup hot enough that the mixture reaches 160 degrees, and you get this smooth, shiny, dense-textured meringue that needs no further cooking.

- Swiss Meringue: Beat sugar and egg whites together over hot water, reaching 160 degrees, to create a firm, stable, fluffy meringue that is ideal as an icing.

Cocoa Meringue Baskets
with Nectarines, Berries and Cream

1½ cups plus 6 tablespoons sugar
3 tablespoons unsweetened cocoa powder
6 large egg whites
3 teaspoons vanilla extract
½ teaspoon (scant) cream of tartar

4 nectarines, pitted, thinly sliced, slices halved crosswise
2 tablespoons crème de cassis (black-currant-flavored liqueur)
1½ cups chilled whipping cream
1 ½-pint basket fresh raspberries
1 ½-pint basket fresh blackberries
Powdered sugar
Fresh mint sprigs

Preheat oven to 200°F. Line 3 large baking sheets with parchment paper. Using 3¼- to 3½-inch-diameter biscuit cutter or bowl as guide, heavily trace 9 circles on each of 2 parchment-lined baking sheets. On third parchment-lined baking sheet and using same guide, trace 10 semicircles. Turn parchment paper over so that marked side is down (circles and semicircles will show through). Whisk 1½ cups sugar and cocoa powder in medium bowl to blend. Using electric mixer, beat egg whites, 1½ teaspoons vanilla and cream of tartar in large bowl until soft peaks form, about 1½ minutes. Gradually add sugar-cocoa mixture and beat until very stiff and glossy, about 4 minutes.

Cut off ⅓ to ½ inch from 1 corner of 1-gallon resealable plastic bag. Scoop enough meringue into prepared bag to fill ¾ full. Twist bag shut above meringue and hold firmly closed while piping. Pipe small dot of meringue under parchment in each corner of baking sheets. Press parchment onto dots to anchor.

To form basket bottoms: Starting in center of each marked circle on 1 baking sheet, pipe meringue in continuous spiral to fill circles completely. Pipe 12 marble-size balls atop edge of each circle. *To form basket sides:* On second baking sheet, pipe meringue atop edge of traced circles to form rings. Pipe 12 marble-size meringue balls atop each ring, spacing about ⅓ to ½ inch apart. *To form basket handles:* On third baking sheet, pipe meringue atop outline of semicircles.

Bake meringues until firm and dry, about 2 hours. Turn off oven; let meringues stand in closed oven overnight to dry completely. (*Can be prepared 3 days ahead. Store airtight in single layer at room temperature.*)

Toss nectarine slices with crème de cassis in medium bowl. Beat whipping cream, remaining 6 tablespoons sugar and 1½ teaspoons vanilla in large bowl until peaks form. Place 1 meringue bottom on each of 8 plates. Place 1 meringue side atop each bottom. Spoon dollop of whipped cream into center of each basket. Top with spoonful of nectarine slices, then a few raspberries and blackberries. Repeat with another layer of cream, nectarines and berries. Dip ends of 1 meringue handle into whipped cream and attach to 1 basket; repeat with remaining handles. Sift powdered sugar over baskets. Garnish with mint sprigs and serve.

8 SERVINGS

Peaches with Shortcake Topping

FILLING

4	cups frozen sliced peaches (about 1¾ pounds), thawed
¼	cup sugar
1	tablespoon fresh lemon juice
½	teaspoon ground cinnamon

TOPPING

1½	cups all purpose flour
4	tablespoons sugar
1½	teaspoons baking powder
½	teaspoon salt
1	cup chilled whipping cream
1	large egg
1	teaspoon vanilla extract
1	tablespoon unsalted butter, melted
½	teaspoon ground cinnamon
	Vanilla ice cream

FOR FILLING: Preheat oven to 375°F. Combine all ingredients in large bowl; toss to blend well. Transfer to 8x8x2-inch glass baking dish.

FOR TOPPING: Sift flour, 3 tablespoons sugar, baking powder and salt into large bowl. Whisk cream, egg and vanilla in small bowl to blend. Add cream mixture to flour mixture, stirring until very soft dough forms. Using ¼-cup measure, drop dough atop filling in 9 mounds, spacing apart. Brush mounds with melted butter. Mix remaining 1 tablespoon sugar with cinnamon in small cup; sprinkle over mounds. Bake dessert until filling bubbles and topping is golden brown, about 50 minutes. Cool 15 minutes. Serve warm with vanilla ice cream.

8 SERVINGS

Post-Soccer Party for Eight

Sliced Tomatoes and Cucumbers

Grilled Hamburgers

Corn on the Cob

Bistro French Fries with
Parsley and Garlic
(page 134; double recipe)

Soft Drinks

Peaches with
Shortcake Topping
(at left; pictured opposite)

Whipped Ricotta with Honey and Mixed Berries

2 cups whole-milk ricotta cheese

4 ounces cream cheese, room temperature

4 tablespoons sugar

3 tablespoons honey

¾ teaspoon vanilla extract

4 cups fresh berries (such as blackberries, raspberries and halved strawberries)

2 teaspoons fresh lemon juice

Blend ricotta, cream cheese, 2 tablespoons sugar, honey and vanilla in processor until smooth. Transfer to bowl. Cover bowl and refrigerate until ricotta mixture is slightly set, about 2 hours. (*Can be prepared 1 day ahead. Keep refrigerated. Stir before using.*) Combine berries, lemon juice and remaining 2 tablespoons sugar in large bowl; toss to coat. Let stand 30 minutes at room temperature. Divide ricotta mixture among 6 wineglasses. Top with berries and serve.

6 SERVINGS

Blueberry Crisp with Oatmeal and Almond Topping

3 ½-pint baskets fresh blueberries

2 tablespoons plus ¼ cup (packed) golden brown sugar

½ teaspoon ground cinnamon

½ cup quick-cooking oats

2 tablespoons all purpose flour

¼ teaspoon salt

2 tablespoons (¼ stick) chilled unsalted butter, cut into small pieces

¼ cup sliced almonds

Nonfat vanilla frozen yogurt

Preheat oven to 350°F. Rinse blueberries. Drain. Place berries in 9-inch-diameter glass pie dish. Sprinkle with 2 tablespoons brown sugar and cinnamon; stir to blend. Let stand until sugar dissolves. Stir oats, flour, salt and remaining ¼ cup brown sugar to blend in medium bowl. Add butter and rub in with fingertips or fork until moist clumps form. Stir in almonds. Sprinkle oat mixture evenly over berries. Bake crisp until berries are bubbling and topping is golden, 35 minutes. Serve warm; top with frozen yogurt.

6 SERVINGS

Fresh Summer Fruit in Ginger-Wine Syrup

1½ cups dry white wine

1½ cups water

9 tablespoons sugar

6 quarter-size pieces fresh ginger

2 medium nectarines, halved, pitted, thinly sliced

2 medium peaches, peeled, halved, pitted, thinly sliced

1½ ½-pint baskets fresh raspberries

6 fresh or dried figs, quartered

Combine wine, 1½ cups water, sugar and ginger in medium saucepan. Simmer over medium heat until reduced to 2 cups, about 16 minutes. Cool. Refrigerate until cold, about 1 hour. Remove and discard ginger.

Place fruit in large bowl. Add syrup; toss to coat. Cover; chill at least 2 hours and up to 4 hours before serving.

6 SERVINGS

Nectarines, peaches, raspberries and figs, swirled in a ginger-wine syrup, make for a cool and exotic dessert.

Chocolate Layer Cake
with Mocha Frosting and Almonds

This special-occasion cake is much easier than its complex flavors would suggest. Cocoa and buttermilk give the cake an interesting twist. Instant espresso power gives the frosting a character boost.

CAKE

1¼ cups cake flour
¾ teaspoon baking soda
¼ teaspoon salt
1⅓ cups sugar
⅓ cup unsweetened cocoa powder
⅔ cup buttermilk
1 teaspoon vanilla extract
10 tablespoons (1¼ sticks) unsalted butter, room temperature
1 large egg
1 large egg yolk

FROSTING

1 tablespoon instant espresso powder or coffee crystals
2 teaspoons vanilla extract
10 ounces semisweet chocolate, chopped
1 cup (2 sticks) unsalted butter, room temperature
1 tablespoon light corn syrup
2 cups powdered sugar, sifted

1 cup sliced almonds, lightly toasted

FOR CAKE: Position rack in center of oven; preheat to 350°F. Line bottom of 9-inch round cake pan with 2-inch-high sides with parchment paper. Butter and flour sides of pan and parchment. Sift flour, baking soda and salt into medium bowl. Whisk ⅔ cup sugar and cocoa in another bowl to blend; add ⅓ cup buttermilk and vanilla and whisk until smooth. Using electric mixer, beat butter in large bowl until fluffy. Add ⅔ cup sugar; beat until well blended. Beat in egg and egg yolk. Add buttermilk-cocoa mixture; beat to blend. Beat in flour mixture in 3 additions alternately with remaining ⅓ cup buttermilk in 2 additions. Transfer batter to pan.

Bake cake until tester inserted into center comes out clean, about 40 minutes. Cool cake in pan on rack 30 minutes. Cut around pan sides to loosen cake. Invert cake onto plate. Peel off parchment paper.

FOR FROSTING: Stir espresso powder and vanilla in small bowl until espresso dissolves. Stir chocolate in top of double boiler set over simmering water until melted and smooth. Remove from over water; cool. Using electric mixer, beat butter in large bowl until fluffy. Add espresso mixture and corn syrup; blend well, scraping down sides of bowl. Beat in melted chocolate,

Cakes

then powdered sugar in 3 additions. If frosting is very soft, freeze until firm enough to spread, stirring occasionally, about 10 minutes.

Spoon 2/3 cup frosting into pastry bag fitted with medium star tip. Slice cake in half horizontally. Place bottom layer on 8-inch cardboard round or 8-inch tart pan bottom. Spread 1 cup frosting over bottom cake layer. Top with second cake layer. Spread remaining frosting over top and sides of cake. Reserve 24 almond slices. Press remaining almonds onto sides of cake. Pipe 12 frosting rosettes around top edge of cake, spacing evenly. Place 2 almond slices in each rosette. *(Can be prepared 1 day ahead. Cover; chill. Let stand at room temperature 2 hours before serving.)*

12 SERVINGS

Make-Ahead Cakes

Don't think you have enough time to create a homemade cake on the day of your party? If stored in an airtight container, an unfrosted and unfilled butter or pound cake will keep at cool room temperature for five to seven days. Or plan even further ahead with these tips.

- Freezing Cakes: Rich, buttery cakes—unfilled, unfrosted and wrapped airtight in layers of plastic wrap and aluminum foil—will keep in the freezer for up to six months; lighter foamy cakes can be frozen for up to two months. For layer cakes, cut the layers (if required) and wrap them separately before freezing.

- Freezing Frosting: A buttery frosting can be frozen in an airtight container for as long as two months.

- Final Assembly: Before filling or frosting a frozen cake, let the icing thaw completely in the refrigerator and let the cake layers defrost completely at room temperature.

Gingerbread Squares
with Honey-Mascarpone Cream

TOPPING

1 8-ounce package mascarpone cheese*
2 tablespoons honey
1 tablespoon fresh lemon juice

CAKE

1¼ cups all purpose flour
2 teaspoons ground ginger
1 teaspoon ground cinnamon
1 teaspoon baking soda
¼ teaspoon ground cloves
¼ teaspoon salt
¼ cup finely chopped crystallized ginger
½ cup vegetable oil
½ cup mild-flavored (light) molasses
½ cup (packed) dark brown sugar
1 large egg
1½ teaspoons grated lemon peel
½ cup boiling water

Powdered sugar

FOR TOPPING: Whisk mascarpone cheese, honey and lemon juice in small bowl to blend. Cover and refrigerate until ready to serve. (*Topping can be prepared 1 day ahead; keep chilled.*)

FOR CAKE: Preheat oven to 350°F. Butter and flour 8-inch square metal baking pan. Whisk first 6 ingredients in medium bowl to blend well; whisk in crystallized ginger. Whisk oil, molasses and brown sugar in large bowl to blend; whisk in egg and lemon peel. Gradually whisk in dry ingredients, then boiling water. Transfer batter to prepared pan.

Bake cake until tester inserted into center comes out clean, about 30 minutes. Cool cake 15 minutes. (*Can be prepared 1 day ahead. Cool completely; cover and store at room temperature.*) Cut cake into squares; sift powdered sugar over. Serve warm or at room temperature with topping.

Italian cream cheese, available at Italian markets and many supermarkets nationwide.

9 SERVINGS

Tropical Lime Torte with Mango Compote

TORTE

- 4 large eggs
- ¾ cup plus 2 tablespoons sugar
- ½ cup fresh lime juice
- 1 tablespoon grated lime peel

- ½ cup dark rum
- 1 16-ounce frozen all-butter pound cake, thawed
- 2 8-ounce packages cream cheese, room temperature

COMPOTE

- ½ cup water
- ½ cup sugar
- ½ cup fresh lime juice
- ½ teaspoon grated lime peel
- 4 large ripe mangoes (5 to 6 pounds), peeled, pitted, diced

  Lime slices

Check the supermarket produce section for fresh peeled and sliced mangoes. You'll need about four cups of sliced mangoes for this torte (pictured on page 160).

FOR TORTE: Whisk eggs, ¾ cup sugar, lime juice and lime peel in heavy medium saucepan to blend. Whisk over medium-high heat until mixture thickens and just comes to boil, about 6 minutes. Transfer lime curd to small bowl; press plastic wrap directly onto surface. Chill until very cold, at least 3 hours and up to 3 days.

Line 9¼x5¼x2¾-inch loaf pan with 2 layers of plastic wrap, leaving long overhang. Stir rum and remaining 2 tablespoons sugar in small bowl until sugar dissolves. Trim brown layer from outside of cake. Cut cake horizontally into 3 equal layers. Beat cream cheese in large bowl until fluffy; gently fold in cold lime curd.

Trim bottom cake layer to fit pan bottom; reserve cake trimmings. Brush layer on both sides with ⅓ of rum syrup. Place in pan; spread 1½ cups lime curd mixture over top. Brush second cake layer on both sides with ⅓ of rum syrup. Place in pan; spread remaining lime curd mixture over top. Brush third cake layer on both sides with remaining rum syrup. Place on lime curd mixture; press to adhere. Press reserved cake trimmings around sides. Cover torte with plastic overhang. Refrigerate torte at least 1 day and up to 2 days.

FOR COMPOTE: Stir first 4 ingredients in large bowl until sugar dissolves. Mix in mangoes. Cover; chill up to 1 day.

Using plastic as aid, lift torte out of pan and unwrap. Cut crosswise into 12 slices. Arrange slices on plates. Top with compote. Garnish with lime slices.

12 SERVINGS

Birthday Party for Six

Blueberry and Orange Layer Cake with Cream Cheese Frosting

CAKE

2½ cups cake flour
2 teaspoons baking powder
½ teaspoon salt
½ cup plus 2 tablespoons (1¼ sticks) unsalted butter, room temperature
1½ cups sugar
3 tablespoons frozen orange juice concentrate, thawed
1½ teaspoons grated orange peel
1 teaspoon vanilla extract
4 large eggs
1 cup whole milk

FILLING

2 ½-pint baskets fresh blueberries
2 tablespoons sugar
1 teaspoon fresh lemon juice

FROSTING

1 8-ounce package cream cheese, room temperature
½ cup (1 stick) unsalted butter, room temperature
3¼ cups powdered sugar
2 tablespoons frozen orange juice concentrate, thawed
1 teaspoon grated orange peel
½ teaspoon vanilla extract
2 ½-pint baskets fresh blueberries

FOR CAKE: Preheat oven to 350°F. Butter and flour two 9-inch-diameter cake pans with 1½-inch-high sides; line bottoms with parchment paper. Sift first 3 ingredients into medium bowl. Beat butter in large bowl until fluffy. Gradually add sugar; beat till blended. Beat in concentrate, peel and vanilla. Beat in eggs 1 at a time. Beat in flour mixture in 4 additions alternately with milk in 3 additions. Divide batter between pans. Bake cakes until tester inserted into center comes out clean, 30 minutes. Cool in pans on rack.

FOR FILLING: Combine berries, sugar and lemon juice in heavy small saucepan. Bring to boil over high heat, stirring until sugar dissolves. Boil until mixture is reduced to ¾ cup, stirring and mashing berries with fork, 8 minutes. Chill filling uncovered until cold, about 30 minutes.

FOR FROSTING: Beat cream cheese and butter in bowl to blend. Beat in powdered sugar in 4 additions, then concentrate, peel and vanilla. Chill until firm but spreadable, about 30 minutes.

For a colorful accent that mirrors the flavors of this handsome dessert, garnish the top with curls of candied orange peel.

Cut around cakes to loosen; turn out. Peel off parchment. Place 1 layer, flat side up, on platter. Spread filling to within $1/2$ inch of edges. Chill 5 minutes. Top with second layer, flat side down. Spread $1/2$ cup frosting thinly all over cake. Spread remaining frosting over. Mound remaining berries on top. *(Can be prepared 1 day ahead; chill. Serve at room temperature.)*

10 TO 12 SERVINGS

Pureed fresh mango gives this cheesecake a light and soft texture and subtle tropical fruit flavor. Remember to start this recipe a day beforehand, since it requires overnight refrigeration.

CRUST

1½ cups graham cracker crumbs
½ cup sugar
6 tablespoons (¾ stick) unsalted butter, melted

FILLING

3 large very ripe mangoes (each about 13 ounces), peeled, pitted, coarsely chopped
3 8-ounce packages cream cheese, room temperature
1¼ cups sugar
2 teaspoons vanilla extract
4 large eggs

Additional mangoes, peeled, pitted, sliced

FOR CRUST: Preheat oven to 325°F. Lightly butter 9-inch-diameter springform pan with 2³/4-inch-high sides. Stir cracker crumbs and sugar in medium bowl to blend. Add melted butter and stir until evenly moistened. Press crumb mixture firmly onto bottom (not sides) of prepared pan. Bake until crust is set, about 12 minutes. Cool completely. Maintain oven temperature.

FOR FILLING: Puree chopped mangoes in processor until smooth. Set aside 2 cups mango puree (reserve any remaining puree for another use). Beat cream cheese, sugar and vanilla in large bowl until smooth. Add eggs 1 at a time, beating well after each addition. Add 2 cups mango puree and beat until well blended. Pour filling over crust in pan.

Bake cake until set and puffed and golden around edges (center may move very slightly when pan is shaken gently), about 1 hour 25 minutes. Cool cake 1 hour. Refrigerate uncovered overnight. Run small knife between cake and sides of pan to loosen. Remove pan sides. Transfer cake to platter. Cut into wedges and serve with sliced mangoes.

12 SERVINGS

1   16-ounce bag frozen pitted dark sweet cherries, halved, thawed,
     undrained
¾ cup sugar
¼ cup kirsch (clear cherry brandy) or regular brandy
¼ teaspoon ground cinnamon
2   tablespoons unsweetened cocoa powder
2   ounces bittersweet (not unsweetened) or semisweet chocolate, chopped
¼ cup (½ stick) unsalted butter, cut into small pieces
2   large egg yolks
1   large egg
2   teaspoons all purpose flour
     Powdered sugar
     Fresh mint

Combine cherries with juices, ½ cup sugar, kirsch and cinnamon in heavy medium saucepan. Stir over medium heat until sugar dissolves. Simmer until sauce thickens and is slightly reduced, about 10 minutes. Using slotted spoon, remove ¼ cup cherries from sauce; drain well. Transfer to work surface and chop coarsely; reserve for cakes. Set aside cherry sauce.

Butter two ¾-cup ramekins or custard cups. Whisk cocoa and remaining ¼ cup sugar in small bowl to blend. Stir chocolate and butter in small saucepan over low heat until chocolate melts and mixture is smooth. Remove from heat; whisk in cocoa mixture. Whisk in egg yolks, then whole egg and flour. Fold in reserved chopped cherries. Divide batter between ramekins. *(Sauce and batter can be prepared 1 day ahead. Cover separately; chill.)*

Preheat oven to 350°F. Bake cakes uncovered until edges are set but center is still shiny and tester inserted into center comes out with some wet batter attached, about 22 minutes.

Warm sauce over low heat. Cut around cakes to loosen; turn out onto plates. Spoon sauce alongside. Sift powdered sugar over; garnish with mint.

2 SERVINGS

Caramelized-Nectarine Shortcakes with Sour Cream

BISCUITS

2 cups all purpose flour

¼ cup sugar

1 tablespoon baking powder

1 teaspoon ground ginger

½ teaspoon salt

½ cup (1 stick) chilled unsalted butter, cut into ½-inch cubes

½ cup whole milk

1 large egg

¼ cup chopped crystallized ginger

FILLING

2 pounds nectarines (about 8 medium), peeled, pitted, sliced

⅔ cup (packed) golden brown sugar

1 tablespoon fresh lemon juice

3 cups sour cream (24 ounces)

⅔ cup sugar

FOR BISCUITS: Preheat oven to 400°F. Line baking sheet with parchment paper. Combine first 5 ingredients in processor; blend 10 seconds. Add butter and blend until mixture resembles coarse meal. Whisk milk and egg in small bowl. Add milk mixture to processor; blend using 5 on/off turns. Add crystallized ginger. Using on/off turns, blend until dough just comes together. Turn dough out onto work surface; knead gently 5 turns. Shape dough into log; cut crosswise into 8 rounds. Pat each round to 1-inch thickness; place on prepared baking sheet.

Bake biscuits until tester inserted into center comes out clean, about 15 minutes. Transfer to rack; cool at least 15 minutes and up to 2 hours.

FOR FILLING: Combine half of nectarines, ⅓ cup brown sugar and ½ tablespoon lemon juice in heavy large skillet. Cook over high heat until fruit is just tender and juices bubble thickly, stirring often, about 5 minutes. Transfer to bowl; repeat with remaining nectarines, brown sugar and lemon juice. Set aside at least 30 minutes and up to 2 hours.

Whisk sour cream and ⅔ cup sugar in bowl to blend. Cut biscuits horizontally in half. Place 1 biscuit bottom in each of 8 shallow bowls. Spoon filling and sour cream mixture onto each; cover each with biscuit top.

8 SERVINGS

Fusion Dinner for Eight

Orange and Red-Onion Salad

Tandoori-Style Grilled Chicken
(page 74)

Steamed Rice

Yogurt with Diced Cucumbers

Beer

Caramelized-Nectarine Shortcakes with Sour Cream
(at left; pictured on page 2)

Old-fashioned Coconut Cake

The secret to this gorgeous yet easy cake? It begins with a mix. Cream of coconut adds tropical flavor to the cake and the cream cheese frosting.

CAKE

- 1   18.5-ounce package butter recipe golden cake mix
- 3   large eggs
- ½   cup (1 stick) unsalted butter, room temperature
- ⅓   cup sweetened cream of coconut (such as Coco López)*
- ⅓   cup water
- 1   tablespoon dark rum

FROSTING

- 2   8-ounce packages cream cheese, room temperature
- ½   cup (1 stick) unsalted butter, room temperature
- ½   cup sweetened cream of coconut
- ¾   cup powdered sugar
- 1   teaspoon vanilla extract
- 1   10-ounce package sweetened flaked coconut (about 3 cups)

FOR CAKE: Preheat oven to 375°F. Butter and flour two 9-inch-diameter cake pans. Combine all 6 ingredients in large bowl. Using electric mixer, beat on low speed until smooth. Increase speed to medium and beat 4 minutes. Divide batter between prepared pans. Bake cakes until tester inserted into center comes out clean, about 25 minutes. Cool in pans 10 minutes. Cut around cakes to loosen; turn out onto racks. Cool completely.

FOR FROSTING: Using electric mixer, beat cream cheese, butter and cream of coconut in large bowl until smooth. Beat in powdered sugar and vanilla. Place 1 cake layer, flat side up, on platter. Spread layer with ¾ cup frosting. Sprinkle with ¾ cup flaked coconut. Top with second cake layer, flat side down. Cover top and sides of cake with remaining frosting. Press remaining flaked coconut over top and sides of cake. Chill cake until frosting is firm, at least 1 hour. *(Can be prepared 1 day ahead. Cover loosely and keep chilled until 1 hour before serving.)*

Cream of coconut is available in the liquor section of most supermarkets.

12 SERVINGS

Spice Cake with Blackberry Filling and Cream Cheese Frosting

Blackberries and a cream cheese frosting turn a familiar spice cake into a sophisticated finale.

CAKE

- 2 cups cake flour
- 2 teaspoons ground cinnamon
- 1 teaspoon baking soda
- ½ teaspoon salt
- ½ teaspoon ground allspice
- ¼ teaspoon ground ginger
- ¼ teaspoon ground nutmeg
- ½ cup (1 stick) unsalted butter, room temperature
- 1½ cups (packed) golden brown sugar
- 3 large eggs, separated
- 1 cup sour cream

FILLING AND FROSTING

- 4 ½-pint baskets fresh blackberries
- ¼ cup sugar

- 1½ 8-ounce packages cream cheese, room temperature
- ¾ cup (1½ sticks) unsalted butter, room temperature
- 5 cups powdered sugar (about 1¼ pounds)
- 2 tablespoons sour cream
- 1 teaspoon vanilla extract

FOR CAKE: Preheat oven to 350°F. Butter and flour 9-inch-diameter springform pan with 2¾-inch-high sides. Sift first 7 ingredients into small bowl. Using electric mixer, beat butter in large bowl until fluffy. Add brown sugar and beat until well blended. Beat in egg yolks. Beat in flour mixture in 3 additions alternately with sour cream in 2 additions. Using clean dry beaters, beat egg whites in medium bowl until stiff but not dry; fold into batter in 2 additions. Transfer batter to prepared pan.

Bake cake until top is golden and tester inserted into center comes out clean, about 45 minutes. Cool cake 10 minutes. Cut around pan sides; release pan sides. Cool cake completely on rack.

FOR FILLING AND FROSTING: Mix 3 baskets blackberries and ¼ cup sugar in bowl. Mash fruit coarsely with fork. Let filling stand at room temperature, at least 20 minutes and up to 1 hour.

Beat cream cheese and butter in large bowl until fluffy. Beat in powdered sugar, then sour cream and vanilla. Cut cake horizontally into 3 equal layers. Place bottom layer, cut side up, on platter. Spread 1 cup frosting over. Spread half of filling (about ¾ cup) over frosting, leaving ¼-inch plain border. Top with second cake layer and 1 cup frosting, then remaining filling. Top with third cake layer, cut side down. Spread remaining frosting over top and sides of cake. Refrigerate until frosting sets, about 1 hour. *(Can be prepared 1 day ahead. Cover loosely; keep chilled until 1 hour before serving.)* Garnish cake with remaining 1 basket blackberries.

10 TO 12 SERVINGS

Flan takes on a Cuban accent with the addition of lemon peel, cinnamon and aniseed.

1½ cups sugar
¼ cup water

1¼ cups whole milk
1½ teaspoons aniseed
1 cinnamon stick
¾ teaspoon grated lemon peel

1 14-ounce can sweetened condensed milk
4 large eggs
2 teaspoons vanilla extract
⅛ teaspoon salt

Stir sugar and ¼ cup water in heavy small saucepan over medium heat until sugar dissolves. Increase heat and boil without stirring until syrup turns deep amber color, occasionally brushing down sides of pan with wet pastry brush and swirling pan, about 10 minutes. Quickly pour caramel into eight ¾-cup ramekins or custard cups. Using oven mitts as aid, immediately tilt each ramekin to coat bottom with caramel. Transfer ramekins to 13x9x2-inch baking pan. Set aside.

Mousses & Puddings

Combine whole milk and next 3 ingredients in medium saucepan. Bring to simmer. Remove from heat. Cover and let stand 45 minutes.

Position rack in center of oven and preheat to 350°F. Pour milk mixture into large bowl. Add remaining ingredients and whisk to blend. Strain egg mixture into another large bowl. Pour custard into prepared ramekins, dividing equally. Pour enough hot water into baking pan to come halfway up sides of ramekins. Bake flans until center is gently set, about 35 minutes. Transfer flans to rack and cool. Cover and chill overnight. *(Can be prepared 2 days ahead. Keep chilled.)*

Run knife around 1 flan to loosen. Invert onto plate. Shake gently. Lift off ramekin, allowing syrup to run over flan. Repeat with remaining flans.

8 SERVINGS

Cherry and Almond Clafoutis

1   16-ounce package frozen dark sweet cherries, thawed, drained
2   tablespoons plus ½ cup sugar
1   tablespoon cornstarch

4   large eggs
1   teaspoon vanilla extract
¼   cup (½ stick) butter
¾   cup whole milk
⅓   cup almonds, toasted, cooled
¼   cup all purpose flour
⅛   teaspoon salt

    Pistachio or vanilla ice cream

Preheat oven to 325°F. Generously butter six 1-cup custard cups. Mix cherries, 2 tablespoons sugar and cornstarch in bowl. Divide among cups.

Whisk eggs, vanilla and remaining ½ cup sugar in medium bowl until well blended. Cook butter in heavy small saucepan over medium-low heat until butter begins to brown, about 3 minutes. Add butter to egg mixture and whisk to blend. Whisk in milk. Finely grind almonds, flour and salt in processor. Stir nut mixture into custard. Pour custard over cherries in custard cups, dividing equally.

Bake clafoutis until set in center, about 35 minutes. Run knife around sides of clafoutis to loosen. Slide out onto plates. Serve clafoutis warm or at room temperature with ice cream.

MAKES 6

Salad of Pears, Blue Cheese and Walnuts

Beef Stew with Winter Root Vegetables
(page 42)

Crusty Bread

Barolo or Red Zinfandel

Cherry and Almond Clafoutis
(at left)

1 cup chilled whipping cream
3 tablespoons amaretto

6 ounces semisweet chocolate, chopped
3 large egg yolks
½ teaspoon vanilla extract
¼ teaspoon almond extract
5 large egg whites
3 tablespoons sugar
6 tablespoons crushed amaretti cookies (Italian macaroons)*

Powdered sugar

Position rack in center of oven; preheat to 400°F. Butter six ¾-cup soufflé dishes; dust with sugar. Place on baking sheet. Whisk ½ cup cream and 1 tablespoon amaretto in medium bowl to soft peaks; refrigerate whipped cream.

Stir ½ cup cream and chocolate in medium bowl set over saucepan of simmering water until melted and smooth. Remove from over water. Whisk in egg yolks 1 at a time, blending well after each addition. Whisk in 2 tablespoons amaretto and both extracts. Using electric mixer, beat egg whites in large bowl until soft peaks form. Gradually add 3 tablespoons sugar, beating until stiff but not dry. Fold whites into chocolate mixture in 2 additions. Spoon enough batter into each soufflé dish to fill dish halfway. Sprinkle each with ½ tablespoon crushed amaretti cookies. Top with remaining soufflé batter. Sprinkle each with ½ tablespoon amaretti cookies.

Bake soufflés until puffed and set, about 13 minutes. Dust each soufflé with powdered sugar. Accompany soufflés with whipped cream. Serve immediately.

Available at Italian markets and some supermarkets nationwide.

6 SERVINGS

Honeyed Panna Cotta
with Dried Figs and Sauternes

1 cup whole milk

1 tablespoon unflavored gelatin

3 cups whipping cream

4 tablespoons sugar

3 tablespoons honey

⅛ teaspoon salt

¼ teaspoon vanilla extract

2 cups Sauternes or Quady Winery Essensia*

8 dried black Mission figs, quartered

Place milk in heavy small saucepan. Sprinkle gelatin over. Let stand 5 minutes to soften. Stir over medium heat until gelatin dissolves, about 5 minutes (do not boil). Add cream, 3 tablespoons sugar, honey and salt and stir until sugar dissolves, about 2 minutes. Remove from heat. Whisk in vanilla. Cool slightly. Strain into 8 wineglasses. Refrigerate until set, at least 5 hours. *(Can be prepared 2 days ahead. Cover and keep refrigerated.)*

Combine Sauternes, figs and remaining 1 tablespoon sugar in heavy medium saucepan over medium-high heat. Boil until mixture is reduced to ¾ cup, stirring occasionally, about 15 minutes. Remove from heat. Cool completely. *(Can be prepared 1 day ahead. Cover and refrigerate.)*

Spoon some figs and cooking liquid atop each panna cotta and serve.

A California dessert wine made with Orange Muscat grapes; available at liquor stores and some supermarkets.

8 SERVINGS

Raspberry-Lemon Trifle

Purchased pound cake makes this trifle easier to prepare. Get started a day ahead of time so that it can chill overnight.

SYRUP

½ cup sugar

⅓ cup fresh lemon juice

¼ cup water

CURD

4 large eggs

1 cup sugar

⅓ cup fresh lemon juice

½ cup (1 stick) unsalted butter, room temperature

1 tablespoon grated lemon peel

FRUIT AND TOPPING

4 ½-pint baskets fresh raspberries

¼ cup plus 3 tablespoons sugar

1 16-ounce frozen pound cake, thawed

2 cups chilled whipping cream

FOR SYRUP: Combine sugar, lemon juice and ¼ cup water in small saucepan. Bring to boil over medium heat, stirring until sugar dissolves. Reduce heat to medium-low and simmer 1 minute. Cover and chill.

FOR CURD: Whisk eggs, sugar and lemon juice in heavy medium saucepan

to blend. Add butter and lemon peel. Stir over medium heat until curd thickens to pudding consistency, about 10 minutes. Transfer to small bowl. Press plastic wrap onto surface of curd. Chill until cold, at least 4 hours. *(Can be prepared 3 days ahead. Keep chilled.)*

FOR FRUIT AND TOPPING: Combine 2 baskets raspberries and ¼ cup sugar in bowl. Mash berries coarsely with fork. Let stand until juices form, stirring occasionally, about 30 minutes.

Cut cake crosswise into 8 pieces. Cut each piece into 3 strips. Line bottom of 3-quart trifle bowl with 8 cake strips, trimming to fit. Drizzle with 3 table-spoons syrup; spread with ⅔ cup curd, then half of mashed berries. Repeat layering. Top with remaining cake, syrup and curd. Cover; chill overnight.

Beat cream and remaining 3 tablespoons sugar in bowl until peaks form; spread over trifle. Mound remaining berries in center and serve.

16 SERVINGS

Ginger Crème Brûlée

3 cups whipping cream
2 tablespoons (packed) coarsely grated peeled fresh ginger
10 large egg yolks
1 cup plus 4 teaspoons sugar
Fresh strawberries
Fresh mint

Accents of ginger and mint lend a clever new twist to a traditional European standby. Bake the custards a day ahead so they chill fully before the topping is broiled.

Preheat oven to 325°F. Combine cream and ginger in heavy medium saucepan. Bring to simmer over medium heat. Remove from heat; let stand 20 minutes. Strain cream into small bowl, pressing on solids in sieve. Whisk egg yolks and 1 cup sugar in medium bowl to blend. Gradually whisk in warm cream. Divide custard among eight ¾-cup ramekins or custard cups. Place ramekins in large roasting pan. Pour enough warm water into pan to come halfway up sides of ramekins.

Bake custards just until set in center when pan is shaken gently, about 45 minutes. Remove custards from water bath; chill uncovered until cold, at least 3 hours. Cover and chill overnight.

Preheat broiler. Place custards on baking sheet. Sprinkle each with ½ teaspoon sugar. Broil until sugar melts and caramelizes, turning sheet for even browning, about 1 minute. Refrigerate custards until topping is cold and brittle, about 1 hour and up to 2 hours. Garnish custards with strawberries and mint and serve.

8 SERVINGS

Berrymisù

This dessert can be quickly garnished with fresh raspberries just before serving.

1   12-ounce package frozen unsweetened raspberries, thawed
12   ounces cream cheese, room temperature
1½   cups sugar
2   cups chilled whipping cream

1   cup water
½   cup fresh lemon juice
40   (about) Champagne biscuits (crisp ladyfinger-style cookies; from two 3.5-ounce packages)

Puree thawed raspberries in processor until smooth. Strain into medium bowl, pressing on solids to extract as much liquid as possible. Discard seeds in strainer. Using electric mixer, beat cream cheese and ½ cup sugar in large bowl until smooth. Beat chilled whipping cream in another large bowl until peaks form. Gently fold whipped cream into cream cheese mixture. Add pureed raspberries and fold just until combined.

Bring remaining 1 cup sugar, 1 cup water and lemon juice to boil in small saucepan, stirring frequently. Cool slightly. Dip 1 biscuit briefly into lemon syrup, turning to coat. Place flat side up in bottom of 12-cup trifle dish. Repeat with enough biscuits to cover bottom of trifle dish, trimming biscuits to fit if necessary. Spread ⅓ of raspberry-cream cheese mixture over biscuits in trifle dish. Dip more biscuits into lemon syrup and arrange atop raspberry-cream cheese mixture in dish, covering completely and trimming to fit if necessary. Repeat layering with more raspberry-cream cheese mixture, then biscuits; top with remaining raspberry-cream cheese mixture. Cover and refrigerate until set, at least 3 hours and up to 1 day.

8 SERVINGS

Coffee-Brandy Crème Brûlée

2 cups whipping cream

¼ cup sugar

1½ teaspoons instant coffee crystals

4 large egg yolks

1 tablespoon brandy

1 teaspoon vanilla extract

3 tablespoons (packed) golden brown sugar

The fabulous texture and perfect balance of coffee and brandy flavors in this custard are enhanced by a crunchy brown-sugar topping.

Preheat oven to 350°F. Arrange six ³/₄-cup ramekins or custard cups in 13x9x2-inch metal baking pan. Combine cream and ¹/₄ cup sugar in heavy medium saucepan; bring almost to simmer, stirring until sugar dissolves. Remove from heat; add coffee and whisk to dissolve. Whisk egg yolks in medium bowl. Gradually whisk in cream mixture, then brandy and vanilla. Strain into 4-cup measuring cup; pour into ramekins, dividing equally. Pour enough hot water into pan to come halfway up sides of ramekins.

Bake custards until center moves only slightly when pan is shaken gently, about 35 minutes. Remove custards from pan. Chill until cold, at least 3 hours, then cover and keep chilled overnight.

Preheat broiler. Arrange custards on baking sheet. Press ¹/₂ tablespoon brown sugar through strainer onto each custard, forming even layer. Broil 6 inches from heat source until sugar bubbles and caramelizes, watching carefully and rotating for even browning, 4 minutes. Refrigerate custards until sugar topping hardens, at least 1 hour and up to 4 hours.

6 SERVINGS

Duo of Chocolate and Cranberry Sorbets

CHOCOLATE SORBET

- 1 cup sugar
- ¼ cup unsweetened cocoa powder
- 3 cups water
- 8 ounces bittersweet (not unsweetened) or semisweet chocolate, finely chopped

CRANBERRY SORBET

- 2 cups fresh or frozen cranberries
- 1¼ cups sugar
- 1¼ cups water
- ½ cup frozen cranberry juice concentrate
- 1 teaspoon fresh lemon juice
- 2 tablespoons grated orange peel

Orange slices or orange peel strips (optional)

FOR CHOCOLATE SORBET: Whisk sugar and cocoa in heavy large saucepan until blended. Whisk in 3 cups water; add chocolate. Bring mixture just to boil over medium-high heat, whisking constantly. Reduce heat to medium; simmer 1 minute, whisking occasionally. Remove from heat; strain into medium bowl. Cool to room temperature. Process in ice cream maker according to manufacturer's instructions. Transfer to container; freeze until solid, at least 6 hours. (*Can be made 1 week ahead. Keep frozen.*)

Frozen Desserts

FOR CRANBERRY SORBET: Combine first 5 ingredients in large saucepan. Bring to boil over medium-high heat, stirring until sugar dissolves. Reduce heat to medium; simmer until cranberries pop and are soft, stirring occasionally, 5 minutes. Puree in batches in blender until smooth. Strain into medium bowl. Mix in grated orange peel. Cool to room temperature. Process in ice cream maker according to manufacturer's instructions. Transfer sorbet to container; cover and freeze. (*Can be made 1 week ahead. Keep frozen.*)

Scoop chocolate and cranberry sorbets into dessert bowls. Garnish with orange slices, if desired, and serve.

6 TO 8 SERVINGS

Dulce de Leche Ice Cream Cake

    5 whole graham crackers, broken up
    ⅓ cup toasted hazelnuts
    1 tablespoon plus ⅓ cup sugar
    ⅛ teaspoon salt
    5 tablespoons unsalted butter, melted

    4 pints dulce de leche (caramel) ice cream
    2 pints strawberry sorbet

  2½   pounds strawberries, sliced
       Purchased caramel sauce (optional)

Preheat oven to 350°F. Combine crackers, nuts, 1 tablespoon sugar and salt in processor. Blend until nuts are finely chopped. Add butter; blend until mixture is evenly moist. Press mixture over bottom (not sides) of 10-inch-diameter springform pan. Bake until golden, 8 minutes. Cool completely.

Slightly soften 1¼ pints ice cream; spread over crust. Freeze until firm, about 1 hour. Slightly soften 1 pint sorbet; spread over ice cream. Freeze until firm, about 30 minutes. Slightly soften 1¼ pints ice cream; spread over sorbet. Freeze until firm, about 1 hour. Slightly soften 1 pint sorbet; spread over ice cream. Freeze until firm, about 30 minutes. Slightly soften 1½ pints ice cream; spread over sorbet for top layer. Cover; freeze until firm, at least 3 hours and up to 1 week.

Stir berries and remaining ⅓ cup sugar in large bowl. Let stand until berries release their juices, about 30 minutes. Cut around cake to loosen. Release pan sides. Cut cake into wedges; arrange on plates. Spoon berries atop wedges; drizzle with caramel sauce, if desired.

16 SERVINGS

Planning to serve a frozen dessert? Brush confusion aside with these simple definitions.

- **Gelato:** Italian-style ice cream made with equipment that stirs only a small amount of air into the mixture during the freezing process—resulting in a dense, luscious consistency.

- **Granita:** Generally based on sweetened fruit juice or coffee. This is made in shallow metal trays; the mixture is regularly scraped during freezing for a pleasingly coarse consistency.

- **Ice Cream:** The classic frozen confection based on cream and/or milk and often egg yolks. U.S. Food and Drug Administration guidelines require that true ice cream contain at least 10 percent milk fat and no less than 10 percent milk solids.

- **Sherbet:** Generally another term for sorbet. In some places, however, sherbets also include milk or egg whites, giving them a smoother, creamier consistency and flavor.

- **Sorbet:** French term for an (almost always) fat-free frozen dessert of pureed fruit, juice and sugar syrup, simultaneously stirred and frozen for a smooth, fine consistency.

- *Sorbetto:* Italian for sorbet.

Ginger, Fig and Cranberry Semifreddo with Blackberry Sauce

This is like a frozen mousse, which helps explain its Italian name: *semifreddo*, or "half frozen." Start preparation a day ahead.

8	large egg yolks
⅔	cup sugar
½	cup dry white wine
2	tablespoons grated orange peel

2¾	cups chilled whipping cream
⅓	cup dried Calimyrna figs, finely chopped
⅓	cup dried cranberries, finely chopped
¼	cup minced crystallized ginger

Blackberry Sauce (see recipe below)

Line 9x5x3-inch metal loaf pan with plastic wrap, extending over sides by 3 inches. Whisk egg yolks, sugar and white wine in medium metal bowl to blend. Set bowl over saucepan of simmering water; whisk egg mixture constantly until candy thermometer registers 160°F, about 5 minutes. Remove from over water. Using electric mixer, beat mixture until cool and thick, about 5 minutes. Beat in orange peel.

Beat chilled whipping cream in large bowl until peaks form. Add egg mixture and gently fold together. Fold in figs, cranberries and ginger. Transfer mixture to prepared pan. Cover with plastic wrap overhang; freeze overnight. *(Can be prepared 3 days ahead. Keep frozen.)*

Turn semifreddo out onto platter. Peel off plastic wrap. Let stand 5 minutes to soften slightly. Slice semifreddo. Place 1 slice of semifreddo on each plate. Drizzle Blackberry Sauce over each slice and serve.

8 TO 10 SERVINGS

Blackberry Sauce

1	16-ounce bag frozen unsweetened blackberries, thawed
¾	cup sugar
2	tablespoons fresh lemon juice
1	to 2 tablespoons brandy (optional)

Puree all ingredients in processor. Strain into medium bowl, pressing on solids to extract as much liquid as possible. Cover and refrigerate until cold. *(Can be prepared 2 days ahead. Keep refrigerated.)*

MAKES ABOUT 2 CUPS

Coffee-Toffee Ice Cream Tart

CRUST AND FILLING

1½ cups finely ground or crushed chocolate wafer cookie crumbs (about 7 ounces)

½ teaspoon ground cinnamon

¼ cup (½ stick) unsalted butter, melted

½ cup coarsely chopped chocolate-covered English toffee bars (such as Skor or Heath; about 4 ounces)

1½ pints coffee ice cream, slightly softened

TOPPING

⅓ cup whipping cream

1 tablespoon unsalted butter

6 ounces good-quality white chocolate (such as Lindt or Baker's), chopped

1 teaspoon vanilla extract

FOR CRUST AND FILLING: Preheat oven to 325°F. Butter 9-inch-diameter tart pan with removable bottom. Mix cookie crumbs and cinnamon in medium bowl. Add melted butter and stir until crumbs are evenly moistened. Press crumb mixture firmly onto bottom and up sides of prepared pan. Bake until crust is set, about 9 minutes. Cool completely.

Sprinkle 2 tablespoons chopped toffee over cooled crust. Spread ice cream evenly in crust. Freeze until firm, at least 4 hours or overnight.

FOR TOPPING: Combine cream and butter in medium saucepan. Bring to simmer. Remove from heat. Add white chocolate; let stand 1 minute. Stir until chocolate is melted and smooth. Mix in vanilla. Let topping stand until cool and slightly thickened but still pourable, about 15 minutes.

Pour white chocolate topping over ice cream tart; tilt pan to cover top of tart completely. Freeze until topping is firm, about 1 hour. Sprinkle remaining toffee over. Freeze until tart is firm, about 4 hours. *(Can be prepared 5 days ahead. Cover tightly and keep frozen.)*

Using small knife, carefully loosen crust from pan sides. Gently push up tart bottom to release tart.

8 SERVINGS

Here's a party-size ice cream sandwich everyone will love. Use two nine-inch-diameter cake pans so that the cookies keep their round shape while baking. And there's no need for last-minute fuss: This can be made up to three days ahead of time.

BUTTERSCOTCH SAUCE

¾ cup (packed) dark brown sugar

½ cup dark corn syrup

6 tablespoons (¾ stick) unsalted butter, diced

¼ cup sugar

¼ teaspoon salt

½ cup whipping cream

1 teaspoon vanilla extract

COOKIES

1½ cups all purpose flour

¾ teaspoon baking soda

¼ teaspoon salt

9 tablespoons (1 stick plus 1 tablespoon) unsalted butter, room temperature

½ cup (packed) golden brown sugar

¼ cup sugar

1 large egg

1 teaspoon vanilla extract

1½ cups semisweet chocolate chips (about 9 ounces)

3 pints chocolate or vanilla ice cream, slightly softened

FOR BUTTERSCOTCH SAUCE: Combine first 5 ingredients in heavy medium saucepan. Stir over low heat until both sugars dissolve. Increase heat and boil until large bubbles break on surface and sauce drops thickly from spoon, stirring constantly, about 2 minutes. Remove from heat; whisk in cream and vanilla (mixture may bubble vigorously). (*Can be prepared 3 days ahead. Cover; chill. Rewarm slightly over low heat before using.*)

FOR COOKIES: Preheat oven to 350°F. Line two 9-inch-diameter cake pans with 1½-inch-high sides with parchment paper; butter paper. Sift flour, baking soda and salt into small bowl. Using electric mixer, beat butter and both sugars in large bowl until well blended. Add egg and vanilla and beat until smooth. Beat in flour mixture. Stir in chocolate chips. Drop half of dough by large spoonfuls into each prepared pan; spread evenly. Bake cookies until light golden, about 18 minutes. Cool cookies in pans on racks. Carefully turn out cookies; peel off parchment.

Place 1 cookie, top side up, in 9-inch springform pan with 2¾-inch-high sides. Drizzle ¼ cup sauce over. Spread evenly with ice cream; drizzle with ½ cup sauce. Top with remaining cookie, top side up; press gent-ly to adhere. Drizzle with 2 tablespoons sauce. Cover pan and freeze

ice cream cake at least 5 hours. Cover and chill remaining sauce. (*Cake and sauce can be prepared 3 days ahead.*)

Cut around cake with small knife to loosen. Release pan sides. Let cake stand until ice cream is slightly softened, about 20 minutes. Rewarm butterscotch sauce over low heat. Cut cake into wedges; serve with sauce.

10 TO 12 SERVINGS

Mocha Ice Cream Sundaes
with Coffee-Caramel Sauce

1 pint vanilla ice cream
1 pint coffee ice cream
1 pint chocolate ice cream
1 cup fresh raspberries
  Coffee-Caramel Sauce (see recipe below)
1 cup chilled whipping cream, beaten to peaks
1 tablespoon finely ground roasted coffee beans

Arrange 1 scoop of each ice cream in each of 6 stemmed glasses. Sprinkle raspberries over ice cream. Pour about 3 tablespoons warm Coffee-Caramel Sauce over ice cream in each glass. Top with whipped cream. Sprinkle with ground coffee beans and serve immediately.

6 SERVINGS

Coffee-Caramel Sauce

1¼ cups water
1 tablespoon instant espresso powder or instant coffee powder
2 cups sugar
3 tablespoons unsalted butter
½ cup whipping cream

Bring 1 cup water to simmer in small saucepan; stir in 1 tablespoon instant espresso powder. Remove from heat. Set espresso mixture aside. Combine sugar and remaining ¼ cup water in medium saucepan. Stir over medium heat until sugar dissolves. Increase heat to medium-high and boil without stirring until caramel is deep amber color, occasionally swirling pan and brushing down sides with wet pastry brush, about 10 minutes. Remove from heat. Immediately add espresso mixture; sauce will bubble vigorously. Stir over low heat until caramel bits dissolve, about 2 minutes. Stir in butter. Cool slightly. Stir in cream. Serve warm. (*Can be prepared 1 week ahead. Cover and refrigerate. Rewarm over low heat just until warm and pourable, stirring frequently.*)

MAKES SCANT 2 CUPS

Rum-Punch Granita

¾ cup peach nectar
¾ cup apricot nectar
¾ cup pineapple juice
¾ cup fruit punch
½ cup dark rum
1 tablespoon fresh lime juice
½ teaspoon Angostura bitters (optional)
Fresh fruit (such as strawberries, peach slices and pineapple spears)
Fresh mint sprigs

To serve as a drink, freeze until slushy but not solid. Look for Angostura bitters in the liquor section of the supermarket.

Combine first 6 ingredients in medium bowl. Mix in bitters, if desired. Pour mixture into 15x10x1-inch baking sheet. Freeze until icy at edges of sheet, about 25 minutes. Whisk to distribute frozen portions evenly. Freeze again until mixture is icy at edges of sheet and overall texture is slushy (for beverage), about 25 minutes longer. Then freeze until mixture is solid (for granita), about 45 minutes. Use fork to scrape granita into icy flakes. Cover and freeze at least 1 hour and up to 2 days. Scoop granita into goblets. Garnish with fruit and mint and serve.

4 TO 6 SERVINGS

Cantaloupe Granita

4 cups chopped cantaloupe
1⅓ cups Asti Spumante (Italian sparkling wine) or water
1 cup (about) sugar
2 tablespoons fresh lemon juice
3 cups cubed assorted melons (such as cantaloupe, watermelon and honeydew)
Thinly sliced fresh mint leaves, plus sprigs of fresh mint

Puree 4 cups cantaloupe in processor. Add wine, ¾ cup sugar and lemon juice; blend until sugar is dissolved. Pour into 9x9-inch metal baking pan. Freeze mixture until partially set, whisking twice, about 2 hours. Freeze uncovered without whisking until completely set, at least 3 hours or overnight. Run tines of fork across surface of granita to form icy flakes. Cover with foil; freeze up to 2 days. Toss melon cubes and up to ¼ cup sugar to sweeten in small bowl. Mound granita in 6 ice-cold Martini glasses. Top with fruit cubes and mint.

6 SERVINGS

Cinnamon-Chocolate Brownies with Chocolate Ganache

BROWNIES

½ cup all purpose flour

1½ teaspoons ground cinnamon

⅛ teaspoon salt

6 ounces semisweet chocolate, chopped

¾ cup (1½ sticks) unsalted butter, diced, room temperature

4 large eggs

1 cup sugar

1½ teaspoons vanilla extract

1 cup chopped walnuts

GANACHE

6 ounces semisweet chocolate, chopped

3 tablespoons unsalted butter, room temperature

2 tablespoons whipping cream

FOR BROWNIES: Position rack in center of oven and preheat to 350°F. Generously butter 8x8x2-inch metal baking pan; dust with flour. Mix first 3 ingredients in small bowl. Stir chocolate and butter in top of double boiler set over simmering water until melted and smooth. Turn off heat. Let chocolate stand over water. Using electric mixer, beat eggs and sugar in large bowl until mixture thickens and falls in soft ribbon when beaters are

Cookies

The Flavors of Bon Appétit 2002

lifted, about 5 minutes. Beat in vanilla. Stir in flour mixture in 2 additions, blending well after each. Gradually add warm chocolate to egg mixture, beating until just combined. Stir in walnuts.

Pour batter into prepared pan. Bake brownies until top is set and tester inserted into center comes out with moist crumbs attached, about 35 minutes. Cool completely in pan on rack.

FOR GANACHE: Whisk all ingredients in small saucepan over medium-low heat until melted and smooth. Pour evenly over brownies in pan.

Chill brownies until ganache is set, about 2 hours. Cut into 16 squares. (*Can be prepared 2 days ahead. Cover; chill. Serve at room temperature.*)

MAKES 16

Peanut Butter and Chocolate "Kiss" Cookies

      1 cup all purpose flour
    ¾ cup whole wheat flour
      1 teaspoon baking soda
    ½ teaspoon salt
    ½ cup (1 stick) unsalted butter, room temperature
    ⅔ cup chunky peanut butter
      1 tablespoon mild-flavored (light) molasses
      1 cup (packed) dark brown sugar
      1 large egg
      1 teaspoon vanilla extract

        Sugar
    48 (about) Hershey's Kisses, unwrapped

Preheat oven to 350°F. Butter 3 large baking sheets. Whisk first 4 ingredients in medium bowl to blend. Using electric mixer, beat butter in large bowl until light. Beat in peanut butter and molasses, then brown sugar. Add egg and vanilla; beat until well blended. On low speed, beat in dry ingredients just until blended.

Roll dough into 1-inch balls. Roll each ball in sugar and place on baking sheets, spacing 1½ inches apart. Bake 10 minutes. Press 1 chocolate "Kiss" into center of each hot cookie, pressing down firmly so that cookie cracks around edges. Bake just until chocolate appears slightly glossy, about 2 minutes longer. Transfer cookies to racks and cool completely. (*Can be prepared 2 days ahead. Store airtight at room temperature.*)

MAKES ABOUT 4 DOZEN

Nonstick Strategies

To grease or not to grease? That is the question facing bakers who worry that their cookies might stick to the baking pan.

The simplest answer is to follow the recipe carefully. Thoroughly tested recipes from reliable sources such as *Bon Appétit* will specify how to prepare bakeware—whether to leave it ungreased; grease it with butter, shortening, oil or nonstick spray; or line it with parchment paper. Bakeware with stick-resistant coatings may help, but don't necessarily always solve the problem. Pans made of two layers of metal with a layer of insulating air between them won't help with sticking; they primarily prevent burning.

Among the best new tools for stick-free baking are flexible, reusable silicone liners reinforced with fiberglass threads, commonly sold under the brand name Silpat. Silpats also keep baked goods from browning too quickly on the bottom. Position a liner with its rougher slip-resistant side down on a baking sheet or in a pan and simply place cookies on top for baking. Once done, the baked goods slip right off the liner, which washes easily with soap and water.

Two Times Is the Charm

Italy's popular crunchy cookies, biscotti, can be the ideal accompaniment to coffee drinks, tea, brandies or cordials. Classic varieties are studded with almonds or hazelnuts, but the cookies may also contain other nuts, chocolate chips, raisins or chopped dried fruit, and may be scented with sweet seasonings such as aniseed and citrus peel. Some elegant biscotti are also dipped partially or entirely in chocolate.

They've come a long way from their origins. Historians speculate that the first biscotti were developed more than five centuries ago as reliable rations for long ocean voyages. That's because, as the literal translation of their Italian name implies, they are "twice-cooked"—first in a loaf form, then as slices. The second baking eliminates virtually all moisture, not only giving them their noteworthy texture but also, as any old Italian seafarer could have told you, helping biscotti keep without spoiling for many months.

Triple-Chocolate Biscotti

1¾ cups all purpose flour
⅓ cup unsweetened cocoa powder
2 teaspoons baking powder
½ teaspoon salt
1 cup sugar
6 tablespoons (¾ stick) unsalted butter, room temperature
3 large eggs
1½ teaspoons vanilla extract
8 ounces semisweet chocolate chips
½ cup white baking chips

Line large baking sheet with 2 layers of foil. Sift flour, cocoa, baking powder and salt into medium bowl. Using electric mixer, beat sugar and butter in large bowl to blend. Beat in eggs 1 at a time, then vanilla. Beat in flour mixture. Stir in semisweet and white chips. Drop dough by heaping tablespoonfuls onto prepared sheet in two 10- to 11-inch-long strips, spacing 3 inches apart. Using metal spatula or wet fingertips, shape strips into 11x2½-inch logs. Refrigerate 30 minutes.

The Flavors of Bon Appétit 2002

Preheat oven to 350°F. Bake logs until tops are cracked and dry and tester inserted into center comes out clean, about 25 minutes; cool 10 minutes.

Reduce oven temperature to 300°F. Using foil as aid, lift logs onto work surface. Line baking sheets with clean foil. Using serrated knife, gently cut warm logs crosswise into ¾-inch-thick slices. Arrange half of slices, cut side down, on each prepared baking sheet.

Bake biscotti until just dry to touch, about 8 minutes. Turn biscotti over. Bake until top is dry to touch, about 8 minutes. Cool on sheets.

MAKES ABOUT 30

Colorado Cowboy Cookies

2	cups all purpose flour
2	cups old-fashioned oats
1	teaspoon baking soda
½	teaspoon baking powder
½	teaspoon salt
1	cup (2 sticks) unsalted butter, room temperature
¾	cup sugar
¾	cup plus 2 tablespoons (packed) dark brown sugar
2	large eggs
1	teaspoon vanilla extract
1½	cups semisweet chocolate chips
1	cup chopped toasted walnuts (about 4 ounces)

These extra-large cookies make a wonderful finish for a casual supper—or an indulgent after-noon snack.

Whisk first 5 ingredients in medium bowl to blend. Using electric mixer, beat butter and both sugars in large bowl until light and fluffy. Add eggs and vanilla, beating to combine. Add dry ingredients and beat until just blended. Stir in chocolate chips and walnuts. Cover dough; chill 1 hour. *(Can be made 1 day ahead. Keep chilled. Let soften slightly before continuing.)*

Arrange 2 racks in center of oven; preheat to 350°F. Butter 2 baking sheets. Form dough into balls, using ¼ cup dough for each. Place on prepared sheets, spacing 2 inches apart. Flatten with hand to 3½-inch rounds. Bake 10 minutes, then rotate sheets. Bake until cookies are golden brown around edges and firm in center, about 4 minutes longer. Cool on sheet 5 minutes. Transfer to racks to cool completely. *(Can be prepared 1 week ahead. Store airtight at room temperature.)*

MAKES ABOUT 20

Index

Page numbers in *italics* indicate color photographs.

Acknowledgments

RECIPES

Bruce Aidells
Alexis, Portland, Oregon
Helene An
Katherine Anastasia
John Ash
Geno Bahena, Ixcapuzalco, Chicago
Melanie Barnard
Nancy Verde Barr
Christophe Beaufront,
    L'Avant-Goût, Paris, France
Rafih Benjelloun, The Imperial Fez,
    Atlanta
Lena Cederham Birnbaum
Carole Bloom
Anthony Dias Blue
Georgeanne Brennan
Minh Bui, Lemon Grass,
    New Orleans
Floyd Cardoz, Tabla, New York
Adel Chagar, Chameau, Los Angeles
Georgia I. Chletcos
Clay Pit, Austin, Texas
Lane Crowther
Michel Del Burgo, Taillevent,
    Paris, France
Jean Louis De Mori, Locanda
    Veneta, Los Angeles

Lori De Mori
Catherine and Ghislain de Vogüé
Brooke Dojny
Jean-Louis Dumonet, Rhône,
    New York
Suzanne Dunaway
Sandy Ercolano
Aaron Ferer, Tuscany, Salt Lake City
Fish, Paris, France
Janet Fletcher
Hiroshi Fukui, L'Uraku, Honolulu
Mary Gareffa
Rozanne Gold
Ken Haedrich
Ruth and Clay Hall
Inez Holderness
Hostellerie Lafarque,
    Pepinster/Goffontaine, Belgium
Sheryl Hurd-House
Philippe Jeanty, Bistro Jeanty,
    Yountville, California
Michele Anna Jordan
Zov Karamardian
Jeanne Thiel Kelley
Kristine Kidd
Elinor Klivans
Tracy Larson, Shamiana, Kirkland,
    Washington
Leslie Mackie

Guy Martin, Le Grand Véfour,
    Paris, France
Mauro Mafrici, I Trulli, New York
Michael McLaughlin
Françoise Meyer
Selma Brown Morrow
Gavin Newsom
Kim Nguyen, Pasteur, Chicago
Olive's, New York
Christine Piccin
Steven Raichlen
Victoria Abbott Riccardi
Rick Rodgers
Marcela Valladolid Rodriguez
Betty Rosbottom
Russian Tea Room, New York
Patti and Michael Ryan
Sally Sampson
Richard Sandoval, Maya,
    San Francisco
Abbie Schiller
Schumachers' Hotel and Restaurant,
    New Prague, Minnesota
Carmen Scott
Sarah Patterson Scott
John Rivera Sedlar
Siam House, Bloomington, Indiana
Marie Simmons
Susan Simon

Tan Dinh, Paris, France
Frances Teasley
Sarah Tenaglia
Mary Tripoli
Joanne Weir
Dede Wilson
Clifford A. Wright

PHOTOGRAPHY

Jack Andersen
Pascal Andre
Noel Barnhurst
David Bishop
Julie Dennis Brothers
Angie Norwood Browne
Wyatt Counts
Richard Eskite
Dāsha Wright Ewing
Leo Gong
Jacqueline Hopkins
Brian Leatart
Ericka McConnell
Pornchai Mittongtare
Scott Peterson
David Prince
Mark Thomas
Véron-Skinner
Rick Szczechowski